Praise for *Jumpstart Learning in Your Kids*

"One of the things that keep you sane once you become a parent is having a good group of parent friends to commiserate with over coffee and at the bus stop. In her new book, *Jumpstart Learning in Your Kids*, parent and teacher Bridget Spackman becomes that important friend, sharing personal stories culled from her own trial-by-fire experiences, providing all of us with the necessary tools to better understand how children develop into independent, resilient learners and how to support and encourage them along the way."

—Dr. Kimberly Kode Sutton, associate professor of education, York College of Pennsylvania

"*Jumpstart Learning in Your Kids* will make parents think differently about how they can support their child's learning in and out of the classroom! Bridget Spackman shares her expertise as both a teacher and parent in a way that makes the information relevant and realistic. All parents should read this book to better understand their child's developmental levels and learn strategies that will increase opportunities for success!"

—Michelle Ferré, Pocketful of Primary

"Supporting children in the classroom and in a home environment are big tasks. In *Jumpstart Learning in Your Kids*, Spackman beautifully brings her experience as a mother and an educator to help you see growing humans from various perspectives. These insights provide more opportunities to understand, support, and love the wonderful children that we have the privilege of raising."

—Juan E. Gonzalez JR., third-grade teacher

JUMPSTART LEARNING IN YOUR KIDS

JUMPSTART LEARNING IN YOUR KIDS

An Easy Guide to Building Your Child's Independence and Success in School

BRIDGET SPACKMAN

CORAL GABLES

Copyright © 2021 by Bridget Spackman.
Published by Mango Publishing Group, a division of Mango Media Inc.

Cover Design & Layout: Roberto Núñez
Cover illustration: 3d_kot/AdobeStock

For permission requests, please contact the publisher at:
Mango Publishing Group
2850 S Douglas Road, 2nd Floor
Coral Gables, FL 33134 USA
info@mango.bz

For special orders, quantity sales, course adoptions and corporate sales, please email the publisher at sales@mango.bz. For trade and wholesale sales, please contact Ingram Publisher Services at customer.service@ingramcontent.com or +1.800.509.4887.

Jumpstart Learning in Your Kids: An Easy Guide to Building Your Child's Independence and Success in School

Library of Congress Cataloging-in-Publication number: 2021931710
ISBN: (print) 978-1-64250-531-3, (ebook) 978-1-64250-532-0
BISAC category code EDU022000, EDUCATION / Parent Participation

Printed in the United States of America

For my loving parents Nomi and Maria Yusafi

TABLE OF CONTENTS

Introduction

A Letter from a Teacher

"What can I do to help my child at home?"

How many times have you silently asked yourself this question after a long day? Maybe you've even asked, or thought about asking, your child's teacher for help. The reality is that many parents have felt this way at some point in their child's life. Feelings of inadequacy or failure often take away any thoughts of reaching out to those around us. Whether you've taken the first step to getting help or have only thought about it, you are doing the right thing. In fact, it takes great courage to be vulnerable with those around us and open up about our uncertainties around parenting and our child's learning. As education continues to evolve and the methods which drive the instruction change, you probably feel overwhelmed and don't know where to start. You are not alone.

As a late bloomer to my education, I didn't graduate college until I was twenty-six years old. By that time in my life, I had already had my first-born, Ian. He was six years old and getting ready to start kindergarten. I interviewed for a few positions and accepted a position as a kindergarten teacher. It was perfect. My little guy and I were starting a new chapter in our lives on the same day, in the very same year, and in the same grade level. For once, I felt as though I was doing something right.

That year I worked hard to step into my new role as a teacher. I started my deep dive into research on strategies for providing good instruction, and I had spent countless hours creating and developing lessons that were hands-on and engaging. I knew that the work that I was putting in was worth it. I wanted nothing more than to be the best teacher I could be for my students, all while working to make a life for myself and for my little boy. It was not going to be easy, but it was the path that I had chosen.

What I didn't realize was how time-consuming work was going to be. I'd spent four years working to learn everything I could about developmental stages and appropriate teaching methods, and yet I felt completely lost that first year. Teachers will often tell you that you are in survival mode that first year, and they are right. I was in survival mode. While I worked endlessly trying to navigate my way through maintaining a kindergarten classroom, the reality was that I wasn't taking those practices home to my own child.

Coming from a single-mother home and raised by a Hispanic family, my upbringing was slightly different from many others. I loved my childhood and my upbringing, but my experiences or lack of experiences offered different perspectives for me. In turn, that same upbringing is what I gave Ian. For me, education was only a focus while I was in the classroom. It was not like my education was not important. It was! My mother always expected me to do my best. I was to behave in school, listen to my teacher, and get good grades. Those were the expectations, but rarely do I remember being read to or sitting down at the kitchen table to do my work. My mother was working hard to make a life for us. She worked long hours and was tired when she came home. Deep down, I knew that I needed to take care of my responsibilities at school so that I didn't have to burden her at home.

During the spring of Ian's kindergarten year, I was scheduled for a conference with his teacher. I remember this day so well. It was right after school. Ian came into my classroom and I had him stay with a teacher who worked right across the hall from me while I met with his teacher for the conference. As I entered the room, I had two colleagues sitting at the table. This was odd, as a conference was typically only held by the classroom teacher. Only a short way through the conference, his teacher informed me that he was not performing as he should be, and it was their recommendation that he be held back in kindergarten. I cried that day. I cried more than I had in years. For the first time, I felt like a failure as a mother and as a teacher. In my hope to make a life for us, I was distracted from the one thing that mattered most to me. How was I a teacher and yet failing my own kindergartener at home?

That first year was hard. I struggled to keep myself afloat, and Ian struggled with reading and writing. Despite the recommendations of my colleagues, I decided to have Ian move on to first grade. It took many years of continuing my profession as an educator, getting married, and having another little boy to convince myself that I was not a bad mother. It had also taken years of teaching experience and working closely with families to realize that I was not alone in my feelings and problems.

The truth is that there are so many families of all sizes, from all backgrounds, that feel the same way. In fact, you probably feel the same way I did. That's why you are reading this book. Regardless of your upbringing and how strongly you believe in ensuring that your child is adequately prepared for school, nothing can prepare you for raising and teaching children. My degree did not prepare me enough. Only time and experience has allowed me to recognize the factors in establishing an effective and supportive learning environment.

Even then, what I did for my first child is incredibly different from what I did for my younger son, and the same goes for my classroom. As a working mother, it is incredibly easy to get caught up in "going through the motions" of everyday life. We forget to stop and really think about each individual and how what we are doing and what we are asking of them is affecting them. The reality of it all is that our kids are not the same. The kids that I teach on a daily basis are not the same. They each have their own uniqueness, their own quirks. What I have to do as a mom and teacher is identify those traits— really pay close attention and learn who they are, so that when it comes time to help them in their learning, when I challenge them to go outside their comfort zone, I am making decisions based on *who* they are versus *what* I have learned in school.

As you read this book, you will find personal stories about my experiences as a mom, my two boys, my husband, my experiences as a teacher, and finally my own upbringing. I do not disclose the names of students, and I have asked permission from my family to share their personal stories. I have always been a strong believer that it is through our personal stories that we make connections and learn. I will share the knowledge I have acquired through personal research, grad classes, and, most importantly, my own life. Raising a child to be successful is challenging, especially as we are all being pulled in so many directions, but it is not impossible. I hope to share my tips, tricks, and practical information so that you can easily begin implementing right away. Keep in mind that so much of what I share in this book are my thoughts and opinions. After years of service in public education, I have found essential components that have been successful for so many kids and families from all backgrounds. I have worked tirelessly to help kids understand the meaning of learning versus simply regurgitating information. Take the information you read here and make adjustments to fit your needs, and, most importantly, the needs of your child. I can assure you that, with time, dedication, and patience, you will begin to see a difference.

Section I

UNDERSTANDING YOUR CHILD

A s a parent, you know your children best during the early years of their lives: you can interpret their gibberish, and you know what they need in order to fall asleep, what soothes their worries, and the little things that bring them the most joy in life. It's an instinct, a sixth sense, a superpower that you gained the day you became a parent.

There were many times during my early childhood when I had the feeling that my mother was watching me, as if she had eyes in the back of her head. She always seemed to know what I was up to or the trouble I was causing. I used to believe she had superpowers; she had mystical abilities to read my mind and see my every move from the other room. Now, as a mother of my own two children and a teacher to seventy-eight kids every year, I have realized that these superpowers are in fact real.

As I got older and matured, my mother's powers didn't seem to be as real. Overnight, it seemed as though I was able to get away with small acts of defiance that would have gotten me in trouble only a few years earlier. What happened? What changed that made the powers go away? Other than age, the only factor that came to mind was the fact that I had started school.

The majority of your child's day is spent at school or participating in other collaborative and/or sports-related activities. Parents spend less time with their children, so they are able to gain more independence and spend time growing in their social skills. Teachers then place it on themselves to *learn* students in order to best serve them while teaching, and suddenly teachers seem to know your child as much as, or even more, than you do.

Very quickly, teachers begin to pinpoint the individual differences that define each child in their class. Teachers learn which kids crave opportunities for creativity or happily immerse themselves in a good book without ever being asked to, but it doesn't take a teacher to recognize this. You undoubtedly can tell what sparks joy in your child. The difference is that teachers have a better understanding of how kids learn. Teachers develop their own expertise in this field and make it their duty to pinpoint what works for each individual child—a superpower of some sort.

Here is the big secret. Kids are not the same. All kids in fourth grade, or all kids who are six-year-olds, are not the same. They don't learn the same way. They don't process information the same way. They don't engage the same way in conversations and thinking. Brain research tells us that this is true. No matter how hard we try to group kids into a category system, it doesn't seem to fit.

I have been blessed with two great boys. Ian is thirteen years old and Blaine is six years old. The two are complete opposites. Ian was a quiet baby who kept to himself and was incredibly timid in social situations. Blaine blasted into this world with a mind of his own, determined to have his way. Ian is a creative soul and enjoys drawing and crafts. Blaine has always been hands-on. A doer. He learns from his experiences and loathes having to sit and practice something.

Two boys who grew up with different experiences and opportunities. Two boys with different personalities and likes and dislikes. Two boys who are different in how they learn. Parents see this, but often feel as though they are not equipped with the right resources or understanding of how to best serve their children academically. Therefore, there is a disconnect between what kids are learning in school and what they are doing at home. This leads to frustration for both parents and kids.

Before digging into strategies to support your child in learning at home, you have to build a foundation of understanding your child as a learner. The four chapters within this section will get you thinking about your child as a learner and as an individual. As you read these chapters, take time to make observations and jot them down. Have conversations that will help you understand where they are in their learning. Before you set your child up for learning, you must first have a deeper understanding of *who* they are.

Chapter 1

ABILITIES AND NEEDS

In this chapter, you will:

- Learn to recognize the developmental stages of children
- Understand that developmental stages are not precise and can vary amongst children
- Recognize the level and characteristics of your child
- Develop methods to encourage and discourage behaviors at home

D uring my early youth, I learned how to ride a bike. I quickly became an expert, partly because my grandmother would force my cousins and me to stay outside playing for the majority of the day. I found that I was out of the training-wheels stage and riding with the big kids before I knew it. The concept of riding a bike is a lot like the abilities we have as individuals and the things we need to be successful in our learning journey.

As with anything in life, we can't run before we learn to walk. I mean, that would be pretty remarkable and would most likely make you a very famous person, but the reality is that life is a progression. How we progress and learn things depends on so many different factors. You may have learned to ride a bike a lot more quickly than I did, thereby refuting my ideas of being an expert at an early age, but we undoubtedly learned how to ride in the same progression of steps.

You may have also started learning to ride a bike using a balance bike versus training wheels, an experience that I never had as a kid. Perhaps your opportunity to learn using a balance bike offered you a different path and progression from mine, but it was still a progression. As I got older, my needs changed, and my abilities changed. I began learning to ride a twelve-speed bike, and suddenly I was braking with my hands instead of my feet.

Learning is the same. The abilities, resources, and experiences available dictate the ways in which we grow and learn. Take the much-debated theory of nature and nurture. Theoretically, in this age-old debate, either nature—genetics—determines who we are, how we behave, and our abilities, or nurture—the environment in which we are raised—has the greatest impact on who we are. I personally believe that it is a combination of the two.

In order to help your child, you have to let go of where your child *should* be and understand where they currently are. Having true knowledge of developmental levels is a great starting point. Think back to all those informational papers and packets your child's pediatrician gave you. You know, the ones that showed age range, characteristics, and a view to where your child would be going? That is what I mean by developmental levels.

I was a kindergarten teacher for four years. After having up to twenty-five five-year-old children in my classroom each day, I grew to understand their personalities and what they were capable of doing. After getting married, my husband and I made the choice to move up north, where he is from, to be closer to his family. I was fortunate enough to find a job as a fourth-grade teacher. The excitement of having a class that was able to be more independent, hold conversations about books, and complete tasks without needing instructions repeated multiple times became more and more appealing in the days leading up to our move. Fast-forward one month into the school year, and I felt like a complete failure. Everything I had originally expected was the complete opposite in real life. My students were struggling with a variety of emotions and developmental changes. In all honesty, I felt as though I was back teaching kindergarten. Until I was given a book called *Yardsticks* by Chip Wood. This book completely changed my perspective, and attitude, when I returned to school. When I took the time to learn about where my students were developmentally, I was better equipped to help them past the difficult moments and find success at what they were doing in class.

As you begin to read about the characteristics of each level in this chapter, keep in mind that I am in no way a psychologist. I have been learning over the course of several years from Responsive Classroom training, brain-based research, and my experience as both a teacher

and a mom. These characteristics may be different between any
two children. You may also find that your child is demonstrating
some of the characteristics but not all of them. This is fine, and,
yes, it is expected. The purpose of this chapter is to offer a guideline
for behaviors you may not be able to explain or may find yourself
getting frustrated with. I encourage you to continue learning about
your child's developmental stages. This will not only benefit your
understanding of where they are and what they are experiencing, but
it will also allow you to develop effective strategies to support your
child every step of the way.

Preschool to First Grade

The early years of education are what we as parents consider the
most critical time in our child's lives. On that first day of school,
you squeeze your child close to you as thoughts of whether they
will like their teacher, will make friends, or the other kids in the
class will be nice to them flood through your head. These first years
will establish your child's perspective on what school is like, and it
is only reasonable to want your child's school life to begin with a
great experience.

On the flip side, parents can feel self-doubt about their abilities and
whether they have done enough. Did I practice letters and sounds?
Does my child know all their numbers? Should I have practiced
handwriting more? Is my child behind? These questions stem from
our own experiences and perceptions of what we believe is happening
behind closed doors, and from our own insecurities as parents.

Kids at this age are learning at a rapid pace; they require supportive
and encouraging environments to help develop their learning. There

are five key elements that I have found through my research and experience as both a teacher and mother that stand out the most.

Routines and Consistency Are Important

At any age, routines and consistency are important. Waking up, you may have a strict routine. You get up, go to the bathroom, grab a cup of coffee, turn on the news. It offers us stability, a sense of what to look forward to, and a feeling of accomplishment that fuels our hearts and minds. The way you drive to work is a routine. Any other route might cause you to be late or get lost. While you may not actively think about the routines and consistency you have in your own life, they are there.

For your child, routines are equally important, especially if your child, like my own first-born, has a difficult time communicating his/her thoughts. Consistency minimizes the struggles that might later cause stress or frustration. It reduces the number of questions you get in a day and replaces them with contentment in what is happening at that very moment. Building these routines and consistency early on begins to train your child in how their everyday life will function. Think about kindergarten; its entire purpose is to help develop routines and consistency for children as they begin their careers in education.

There is such a thing as too much consistency in our routines. Dictating every minute of each day can be overwhelming and limit the amount of creativity that you allow your child. Create blocks of time that are focused on specific areas. For instance, you may have an hour blocked off for creative arts. Another hour blocked off for play. By doing this, you are giving room for flexibility and alleviating the stress of having to stick to the schedule.

Adaptable to Change

Change is inevitable; this is something we will constantly have to adjust to throughout the course of our lives. Learning to cope with and adjust to change can be challenging, but during these early stages of development, it can be beneficial to begin introducing change to your child. My experience is that children are incredibly resilient, but they are also highly inquisitive. Allow your child to ask you questions, make observations on the change that is happening, and discuss the positives that change can offer. The more we expose our children to change, within reason, the easier it will be for them to develop positive coping mechanisms and responses as they get older.

To introduce change to your child, find a new location away from your home where they can participate in minor activities. Locate a new group of peers who can engage your child in a variety of situations and conversations. Above all else, your child will feel more comfortable with being independent when their needs are being met emotionally at home. Be sure to discuss and make your child aware that you are there to help them grow.

Hands-On

Kids at this age thrive in an environment where they can be hands-on. They enjoy getting messy and exploring with a wide range of materials. Opportunities to explore using their five senses allows them to target various sensors in their brains and develop meaningful connections. Give your child as many opportunities as possible to be hands-on and explore using their senses. These are things they can manipulate, move, and change the form of while exploring a variety of textiles.

When I first started teaching, I thought that hands-on experiences required spending an arm and a leg on various materials, but the truth is that being hands-on does not mean you have to spend an endless amount of money creating elaborate experiences. You would be surprised at the types of activities you can create with just some simple household items. For example, spray some whipped cream or spread a thin layer of rice on a baking sheet for writing letters or drawing shapes. Find objects in nature that allow your child to explore textures or learn to categorize based on shape, color, or other characteristics. Any opportunity you can offer your child to explore how objects work and move can offer great learning experiences that will help them in the future.

Explore Their Surroundings

Learning at this age is about experiencing the environment around them. Looking for words in authentic areas, talking, and sharing questions and information about the spectacular things the world holds can offer your child a wealth of learning opportunities that are authentic and relatable. Think back to when your child was just beginning to crawl and stand up. They were most likely getting into everything in the house. This natural period of exploration encourages your child to learn. Chances are your child was able to identify which areas were dangerous and which were safe.

Take opportunities to explore your neighborhood. Look for various treasures that can offer an opportunity for conversation. Allow your child to explore the environment with their five senses when it is safe and have them share the excitement of what they learned with you. I often took my kindergarteners along the perimeter of our building at school. We would explore various locations, from the garden, pond, and playground, to the track field and more. To encourage kids to take their observations back to the classroom, we would take pictures of various things or fill a basket with collected treasures. Create fun writing or word-matching activities as a way to spark learning. This will not only get them excited about reading, writing, and math, it will also help them make important connections between what they learn at school and their own lives.

Conversations

Kids are curious individuals and often need to process what they are observing or experiencing. The power of conversation can be beneficial at this stage, but it is also important that we encourage the development of conversation. Teaching kids to articulate their thinking in a calm and comprehensible manner will greatly benefit them as they get older.

These early stages of child development are about having kids hold conversations with their peers and with adults. It can be challenging for some kids to articulate what is going on in their heads, especially if a child is learning two or more languages. Using images and giving kids a sentence starter can be very helpful. For example, ask your child a question and help them with setting up the sentence to respond. Encourage them to repeat their sentence, if needed, to make it sound more conversational. Having kids repeat your words is like giving them a head start during a race. Be careful not to make grammar corrections at this stage. Instead, be strategic and repeat what your child is saying by asking for confirmation. If your child says, "I like play at the park," you can say back, "Oh! You like to play at the park? That's great!" This method will continue to encourage their conversation while giving them an opportunity to hear the correct way to say the sentence. The more you say it correctly for them, the more likely they will use it in the future.

Second to Third Grade

Second and third graders begin to embrace their independence and curiosity with an eagerness to engage and participate in new experiences with their peers. At these stages, kids are full of energy and have an innate curiosity about the world around them. They enjoy being at school with their peers and are transitioning from being timid individuals to walking out the door excited for the adventure the day holds. They have confidence and competence in their ability to learn new tools but can become impatient if they are unable to be successful immediately.

While their curiosity about the world and their abilities increase, they may be transitioning from playing with everyone to homing in on a few good friends; however, these relationships can change often. School is still considered a place of learning and exploration. They have a genuine love of learning and want to expand on their own interests. As your child enters into these stages, be mindful of the following characteristics.

Sensitivity

Understanding children who are sensitive can be challenging, and parents need to balance the fine line between firmness and understanding. During these particular years, children may be more sensitive than they are in other years. Tears make a frequent appearance, and feelings are often hurt even if that wasn't the intention. Meltdowns may seem frequent, and their level of empathy increases for others around them. When children show sensitivity in their emotions, that is proof that their brains are developing appropriately.

Be patient during these times. Frequent tears can cause parents to get frustrated or to target their children for being too emotional. This is a time to nurture the emotions and offer time for your child to express their feelings. Listen without offering advice in the beginning. Many times, children need the chance to be heard and express themselves. Allowing this now will let the relationship continue to evolve and develop as your child gets older and begins dealing with more difficult situations.

Perfectionism

Children at these stages are acutely aware of how they compare to other children around them. They become increasingly critical of themselves and often look to be perfect the first time around. This new sense of perfectionism can cause them to feel increasingly stressed when working on assignments at home or thinking of an upcoming test; however, they may also willingly accept feedback from adults to make changes in their work.

Avoid comparing your child to other children their age or those they associate with. Be specific in the praise you give them, and listen intently to their feelings. It is okay to encourage high standards, but be sure to explain that there is a difference between good-quality work and perfectionism. Promoting a few relaxation techniques as strategies can help to calm your child and focus their attention on pursuing the task to completion. Before beginning an assignment, have your child participate in a few deep-breathing exercises, locate a spot that is comfortable, or even find music that encourages relaxation.

Quickly Changing Moods

Moods can change drastically from one moment to the next. During this developmental period, children are learning to regulate the emotions they are feeling. They could very easily dislike their peers one day and be best friends the next. For the most part, children are able to bounce back and continue on with a normal day even after having a meltdown only moments before.

During this stage, refrain from taking anything personally. Give your child time to calm down and think about their feelings. Generally, when given the time and space to reflect and work through their emotions, children are able to realize how they are reacting and correct it themselves. On some rare occasions, you may have to intervene and help your child work through their moods. You may need to provide frequent breaks to help your child with appropriate strategies.

Directions

Remembering directions can be a challenge for children in this age group. Homework, materials, and simple directions are forgotten in less than a minute. Children will struggle with following directions that have more than one step, and when an extended period has passed between the direction and the action. For most parents, their immediate reaction is that their child is not listening to the directions, when in reality the cause is the developmental stage and not the child's listening skills, in most cases. This can lead to you and your child feeling frustrated.

Develop a system with your child. Stick to giving simple, one-step directions, instead of a list of items that need to be accomplished. Also, try not to be too wordy. The more simply you can say the directions, the easier it will be for your child to follow through. One strategy that may be beneficial is to have your child repeat the directions back to you. This will give them an opportunity to use two learning methods: listening and speaking. If you find that homework is a challenge, work with your child's teacher and your child to develop a system that will work for everyone.

Empathy and Equality

Children in these stages of development begin to make a shift from looking inward to having a greater sense of others' feelings. They develop a strong sense of what is right and what is wrong, and they will often tell adults about what others are doing out of concern. Their moral sense and interest in fairness begins to grow, and these newly developed feelings can heighten their emotions and sensitivity.

Take time to discuss empathy by reading books and discussing various scenarios with your child. Follow up with opportunities to help others and encourage your child to connect the feeling to the behavior. Empathy and understanding equality take time to develop when the seed is nurtured. By modeling relationships, communication, and a whole lot of patience, your child will continue to take these opportunities to create new conditions in their brains for empathy and equality.

Fourth to Sixth Grade

Fourth through sixth grade is a time when children begin to fracture into a variety of groups. Unique personalities and friendships define these next stages of development. Children at these ages are working to determine who they are as individuals and immersing themselves in their interests. Often you will notice your child may become increasingly focused on a specific topic or theme. Fictional characters in games and in stories become important, and, for most, school transitions from a place of learning and exploration to a place for social gathering.

Once driven and encouraged by their imaginations, some children will begin to focus on the real world around them. These stages are the beginning of an increasingly difficult period for children. Developmental stages can vary tremendously, and children can show maturity while others are still grasping at their childhood. Children will continue to look for confirmation and approval from the adults around them. It may seem as though, one moment, your child displays younger tendencies and in the next, quickly changes to a mature person.

Emotions

As children in these stages of development begin to change, their emotions are heightened to various levels. There may be times when they cry over the smallest of injuries or over what someone has said to them. As their bodies continue to develop and change, many children are working to process their emotions. These may, at times, seem out of their control, and it is important to not make matters worse by pushing them off.

Encourage your child to talk about how they are feeling. It may be helpful to have a daily check-in using colors or emoji faces to represent emotions. Reassure them that what they are feeling is normal for their age. Give your child some helpful tips for how to cope with various emotions. Also, be sure to talk with their teacher about strategies you may be using at home. Fostering a positive environment for children to express their emotions without being criticized or teased will ensure that your child will be able to cope with various challenges.

Friendships

Friendships are increasingly important at these stages of development. Your child has found their *group* that they feel comfortable with and are beginning to define a few best friends. School becomes a place to interact socially with others and that begins to hold greater importance than the content that is being taught. These stages are perfect opportunities to have kids engage in group activities. They are able to work in a variety of peer configurations and enjoy both competitive and noncompetitive tasks. Kids at these stages are quick to get angry at their peers but are also quick to resolve issues.

Encourage kids to develop friendships by offering opportunities for peers to get together outside of school. Help your child create a variety of friendships by getting together with people from different social groups. For example, you may have a church group that you can set up playdates with, neighborhood friends that you can encourage them to play with after school, or even a sports team that can offer opportunities to hang out and socialize outside of practice. The more opportunities your child has to interact and be social with a range of children, the more accepting and mindful they will be when interacting with others who do not always have the same interests.

Anxiety

Children at these stages become increasingly anxious as they begin
to understand the world in an entirely new light. With a clear
understanding of the events occurring around them, kids begin
to worry about world events and how they may impact them and
others around them. Children will also begin to worry about moving
away, losing friends, or even changing schools. Their feelings of
anxiousness may affect their ability to complete assignments, and
they may worry about upcoming tests or big projects.

When children are demonstrating signs of anxiousness, encourage
them by taking time to listen to their concerns and feelings. Try to
understand their perspective on the situation and offer insight from
a different perspective. Children thrive on the lightheartedness
of adults, and often humor will help them when working through
their feelings.

Rules and Logic

Children at these stages of development enjoy learning about
rules and logic. Lost are the days when the rules of a game would
consistently change to benefit the youngest players. Children in these
developmental stages are attuned to ensuring the rules are being
followed by everyone. They are naturally inquisitive about scientific
principles and the systematic solving of a variety of problems. This
new focus causes them to wonder, argue, and question the world
around them. They enjoy learning about how things work and
engaging in complex tasks.

Encourage your child to engage in a variety of brainteasers and
puzzles. A simple way to encourage students to use logic is by having
them solve math problems backward or by eliminating certain pieces

of the problem. They will use their knowledge to determine the missing parts. Offer children the opportunity to help with putting things together around the house. This might be building a new piece of furniture or taking a large device apart for repair.

Questions Adults

As children enter into fourth grade, they begin to question the world that adults have created for them. They become aware of situations occurring around them, and this new realization piques their curiosity and encourages them to process information. Their questioning allows for meaningful connections to be made and for an increase in their cognitive thinking abilities.

During these times, be patient and explain things clearly. Use simple language and, when possible, show examples. The more concisely you are able to explain the answers to their questions, the more opportunity your child will have to make deep connections. It may be possible to see more behaviors arise at home than at school. Do not take this personally, but rather have conversations about what you are noticing and how you would like to help.

Middle School

Known as the awkward stage in early adolescence, children at this period in their life are working through various emotions and identifying their place in the world. As walking contradictions, they want your love but prefer that you don't show it in public; and as their bodies begin to change, many are struggling to sort through the emotions they are experiencing. Friendships are defined at this point in their lives, and they are working to establish their independence.

Responsibilities begin to increase as the majority of children are transitioning to a school system where they have to manage more than two teachers.

Independence can fool parents into allowing their child to make choices without them, but the degree of a child's success is directly connected to parents who are consciously involved in their growing teen's life. Know what is happening in their lives without wanting to control every aspect. You will find a balance between the independence your teen craves and the support and guidance they need.

Independence

Young adolescents begin to form a growing sense of independence during middle school. They enjoy talking in adult language and being a part of the conversation. As their maturity continues to develop, many adolescents will develop adult personalities. They are ready to embrace their freedom and take on a new role as their bodies and minds are working tirelessly to develop into teens.

Be patient with your developing teen during the middle-school years. Encourage them to be a part of the conversation and use this as an opportunity to develop important communication skills. Take time to discuss making eye contact, listening thoughtfully to the conversation, and being able to make comments and ask questions on what is being discussed. The more you practice these skills, the more it will ultimately benefit them as they continue to get older.

Responsibility

Responsibility is something that can start at a very young age.
Children can be responsible for cleaning their rooms and for
ensuring they have everything they need ready for school the next
day. However, as they grow into the early years of adolescence, they
are able to take on much larger responsibilities. With their growing
sense of maturity, they are eager to take on jobs such as mowing,
babysitting, and more. As their minds and abilities continue to
expand, they become more capable at managing projects that spread
over the course of several days.

Offer your child opportunities for responsibility around the house
or to assist neighbors or other family members. These occasions will
contribute to their feelings of self-worth, as they see themselves as
contributing members of their community and their family. Avoid
looking at these tasks as things they *should* be doing, and instead
focus on helping your child take charge in their life.

Opinions

With their growing awareness of world issues and developing
personalities, young adolescents begin to develop strong opinions.
While they are able to see both sides of an argument, most will
continue to only argue one side. They will also place the opinions of
their friends and peers on a much higher level of importance, and
these can sometimes conflict with your own thinking. You may
find that one moment, your growing teen loves to watch a particular
show, but the moment a friend comes over, they deny or tease
everyone in the family for watching.

It is important to maintain a sense of humor in these situations.
Think back to your own adolescence and recall the passion you felt

for various topics or arguments. It may be hard to keep your cool with certain topics, but acknowledge the way they feel and leave it at the resolution of *agreeing to disagree*. Listen carefully, without judgment or, in my case, facial expressions, as these can trigger some kids to become very defensive. Offer your advice when asked, and know that these opinions can and will change at the drop of a hat.

Isolation

During these stages of development, young adolescents may begin to shut down and withdraw from you and other members in the family. Like hibernating, they may spend more time in their rooms and begin cutting themselves out from family conversations. Music becomes the gateway for many to express their feelings, and seemingly overnight, they might be constantly walking around and listening to their music in the home. As their brains continue to develop, you will find that your young adolescent begins to stay awake later into the evening and sleep in more.

The behavior of isolation is common among children this age. To combat this inward-pulling force, get your child involved in after-school activities, or find programs that allow for social gatherings. Get your child involved in chores and responsibilities at home that require them to be out and about, conversing with others in the family. Find local recreational camps or programs that get your child involved during the summer months and stay active with family members who live nearby.

Friendships

Young adolescents look to their friends for comfort and to confide their feelings. They will want to spend more time with their peers and less time with their families. As kids in these stages are working to process their emotions, many of the friendships that have followed them through elementary school could very well not last through middle school. With rising tempers, and as varying interests and passions begin to emerge, don't be surprised if your child is experiencing some trouble in the friendship department.

Be a source for listening and acknowledging how your child feels during these times. Stay involved by asking questions and being genuinely interested in what is happening. Try to stay away from acting as the accusatory parent, as this may send up alerts in your child's brain that you do not trust them. As much as you may want to offer advice, offer your ear instead, without trying to completely fix the problem. Your listening can often be more valuable than your advice.

The more we are able to observe, listen to, and empathize with our children, the more we are able to truly understand their needs. Children yearn for the opportunity to be understood and guided through the various emotions and changes they undergo. Our job as their parents is to listen and help them navigate through this journey in life. Keep in mind that, while we may want our children to be at a particular point in life, each child is unique and reaches different stages at different times. Give grace to your child as they experience the various stages in development and remember to have patience.

Chapter 2

How Much Is Just Right?

In this chapter you will:

- Develop a deeper understanding of how students are utilizing time in schools

- Understand the amount of time needed for instructional purposes

- Identify the elements that help structure the time effectively

- Develop appropriate times for homework and schoolwork at home to support your child's learning

ave you ever heard the story "Goldilocks and the Three Bears"? It's the tale of a little girl named Goldilocks who walks into the home of three bears living deep in the woods. She enters the house and begins trying out each of the three bears' chairs, food, and beds. Each time she tries something new, she hopes to find the one that is *just right*. Have you heard of it? Great! Think about how often you try things to find the one that is just right for you. Walking into a store to find the right pair of shoes, looking for pants that fit just right, and finding the right tool in order to get the job done. While we are not breaking into the homes of strangers, we are a lot like Goldilocks. We look for objects that fit who we are and how we function.

Just as Goldilocks searched for things that were just right, finding the right amount of time to complete tasks or new learning is essential. Take vacuuming a rug compared to vacuuming a two-story home that is completely covered with carpet in every room. The time needed to vacuum the single rug is going to be far less than that needed to vacuum a two-story home. Time and learning work the same way; we have to be mindful of how long tasks could possibly take, depending on the various needs of your child.

During my sixth year of teaching, I had a challenging schedule. It seemed as though I had a revolving door; kids were constantly coming in and going out to meet with other teachers in the building. Finally, after months of trying to make it work, my team and I decided to create individual schedules for each kid. Picture an itinerary for the day. The schedule would define what kids were supposed to be doing, where they were going to do the task, and how long they had to complete the task. We rolled this out in January of that school year. As the year came to an end and we had spent five months using these schedules, we reached out to our students and families for feedback. We quickly learned, from our observations and from the input of our students and families, that the schedules were great for some, but challenging for others. Why? Well, not every kid is able to complete tasks in twenty minutes.

To understand how learning and time interact, and to give you a better understanding and perspective of what education looks like in a school setting, let's dig deep into a typical school day. It's helpful to have a clear picture of what your child is doing in school so it can transfer to home or another learning environment.

Kids spend, on average, six to seven hours at school, and this does not include travel time. During this chunk of time, they participate in numerous activities, ranging from core subject areas, like math and reading, to extracurricular activities such as chorus, musical instruments, and code. As parents, our perception of school is that kids are being taught information and then have a small amount of time to work. However, this is not the case. In fact, learning in a school setting has changed tremendously, due to college and career readiness standards.

These standards outline the required knowledge and skills students will need in order to be college- and career-ready. This will include soft skills such as collaboration, problem-solving, time management, perseverance, and citizenship. In order to effectively develop these skills, learning has changed from being teacher-focused to being student-focused. This means that the majority of learning is coming from the activity of the student and not the teacher, thus giving students the majority of the day to explore, interpret, collaborate, and practice these skills. Students are seen as the drivers of their learning, and teachers now assume the role of a guide. Knowing this, let's now take a look at a typical schedule for various age levels.

Kindergarten		Fifth Grade	
7:30am - 7:50am	Arrival/ Morning Work	8:40am - 9:10am	Arrival/ Announcements
7:50am - 8:05am	Announcements	9:10am - 9:30am	Morning Meeting
8:05am - 9:05am	Language/ Writing	9:30am -10:40am	Math Block
9:05am - 9:35am	Reading Block	10:40am - 11:30am	Recess/ Lunch
9:35am - 10:05am	Specials	11:30am - 11:50am	Choice/ Flex Time
10:05am - 11:05am	Reading Block	11:50am - 1:20pm	ELA Block
11:05am - 11:25am	Recess/ Bathroom	1:20pm - 2:20pm	Integrated Content
11:25am - 11:48am	Lunch	2:20pm - 3:00pm	Specials
11:55am - 12:35pm	Math Calendar/ Math Talks	3:00pm - 3:30pm	Read Aloud
12:40pm - 1:10pm	PE	3:30pm - 3:45pm	Dismissal
1:10pm - 2:05pm	Math Block		
2:05pm - 2:45pm	Science/ Social Studies		
2:45pm - 3:02pm	Read Aloud/ Dismissal		

Average Schedule for Students

Looking at these numbers, students have around four and a half hours of instruction with their content teacher(s). The remaining time is spent either on specials, lunch, recess, or other extracurricular activities. While all of these are important for the growth of your child's social and emotional skills, it can be an eye-opener for many families to really see how much time is actually spent learning math, reading, writing, social studies, and science. Within each of these core subject areas, the time a teacher spends

giving direct instruction can vary. Let's look at an example of three
grade levels during a typical math block.

MATH BLOCKS

Kindergarten	Third Grade	Fifth Grade
TOTAL TIME: 1 hour 30 minutes	TOTAL TIME: 1 hour 15 minutes	TOTAL TIME: 1 hour 10 minutes
• 15 minutes calendar and math songs	• 10 minutes daily math warm-up	• 10 minutes talks (mental math)
• 10 minutes number talks	• 15 minutes math lesson	• 20 minutes math lesson
• 15 minutes math game	• 45 minutes math practice through stations	• 20 minutes independent practice
• 45 minutes math stations	• 5 minutes share time	• 15 minute spiral practice
• 5 minutes closing circle		• 5 minute closing

Example Math Blocks for Kindergarten, Third Grade and Sixth Grade

Looking at the image above, it's important to notice that the majority
of the time dedicated to math in all three grade levels will be spent
with students working either independently or collaboratively. This
means that students are practicing the current skill or previous skills
during these times. As students work, teachers are offering support
and guidance where needed. Some teachers will make observations
and ask guiding questions, while others may pull students away to
practice more on essential skills. The true amount of instruction is
no more than 40 percent of the class period, and this is including the
whole group practice of all students and small-group instruction that
is teacher-directed.

So why is the amount of instruction a teacher gives so little? Teachers
are ensuring that they are scaffolding the content appropriately
for students and that the children are utilizing a range of higher-
level thinking skills. The goal of scaffolding is to develop a strong

understanding of the basic skills and get kids to incorporate that
learning into more challenging and critical thinking opportunities.
Plus, the goal of any teacher is to never overwhelm students with
learning. Imagine attending a full-day seminar. By the end of the
day, your brain almost feels as if it physically hurts. You struggle to
find words and recall all the information that you learned. With still
young and developing minds, too much information can deter the
process of learning. Now the question remains: What are students
doing with the other 60 percent of their time in each block?

The focus of the 60 percent time block is for students to practice and
apply new or previously worked on skills. This time may be split
between working with peers on projects and completing independent
practice. Teachers offer opportunities to explore skills using hands-
on materials and technology and to work on real-world problems that
encourage the process of design and inquiry. If, during this time, a
child is struggling in an area, a teacher may pull them aside and offer
more guided instruction to reinforce skills. This is also a time for
students to meet with teachers in individual conferences to discuss
progress, set goals, and review assignments.

During my first year teaching fourth grade, I had no idea
how to begin teaching my students to write. In fact, I didn't
even know what writing was supposed to *look* like at that
age. I worked with several teachers and did my research
prior to the start of school. Surprisingly, I found that there
were countless approaches that teachers were taking
to give writing instruction; from telling kids to complete
an entire writing in a day to editing every sentence for
them. All approaches, while intentions were good, did
not seem to work for what I understood or believed about
teaching. I turned to the writing process for help. I used
what I knew about good teaching practices and about

developing authentic opportunities and choice. I broke the lessons down and offered support and practice before expecting my students to pull stories out of thin air. After all, generating a story and articulating it in the form of writing is hard. I quickly found that the more I was able to break down large concepts, the better my students were at understanding and applying them.

Now that you have a better understanding of how students are spending their time at school, the expectation is not to replicate the experience, but to take away the understanding that students are not constantly being talked to during the day, nor are they expected to sit quietly working alone. Teachers work to offer a wide range of opportunities to engage, encourage learning through cross-curricular connections, and encourage students to build essential life skills.

Fortunately, you do not have to worry about managing so many kids in one space, but take away the structure more than anything else— beginning with a quick review of old skills, giving a small lesson that focuses on a specific and attainable learning target, and finally offering ample opportunity to practice new and old skills. This structure will benefit you whether you have decided to homeschool, continue learning over the summer, or establish a homework routine.

Factors that Dictate Time

It would be a perfect world if we could pinpoint the exact amount of time that is perfect for children to learn. However, the concept of time and learning is more complicated than we think. In fact, the appropriate time for tasks and for learning to take place can vary greatly. You know that no two kids are alike. You can see this in your own family and others around you. This does not mean that your child is behind or not progressing the way the brochure tells you. It simply means that your child is just as unique in how they learn as every other kid on this planet.

There are multiple factors that play a role in deciding the amount of time it takes for learning and/or tasks to be completed. As adults, we may even still struggle with some of these factors—I know I do. What's important in moving forward is to recognize the impact that these factors can have in hindering our abilities, but also to recognize the strategies and methods that can be applied to help your children with this process. Understanding is half the battle; taking logical and meaningful steps to help your child can ultimately win the war.

Background Knowledge

Your past experiences and the knowledge you have acquired over the years serve as the stepping stones for gaining new information. The beauty of life is that we are all unique, and we have all experienced life in various ways. The way I experience and perceive life is vastly different from the way my husband was raised. In fact, the ways my two boys were raised are also incredibly different.

Our lives evolve, and with that come different opportunities. These opportunities lead to experiences that allow us to make connections later on in life. Everything we learn and take in from our world around us *sticks* because of the connections our brain makes. When we cannot make connections and understand why information is important or relevant, then we struggle to remember the information later on.

Before sitting down to start a new learning topic or to work on homework, you need to determine how much your child knows about this. This is what teachers in education refer to as schema; these are the file folders in our brains where we store information. This can happen in a number of ways: have your child write down everything they remember from the lesson prior to this one or what they know about the concept. For example, if your child is learning to add and subtract fractions with uncommon denominators, you may begin by asking what they know about fractions in general. This will give you a clear starting point for what they understand and what you may need to review.

The level of understanding and whether or not your child has enough information on the topic will be among the deciding factors in how long learning may take. A child who has significant understanding on a topic may be able to make connections more quickly than another child.

I had the privilege of providing math instruction to a well-respected colleague's son. He was a third grader and came to me to learn fourth-grade math. Coincidentally, his brother was also in my math class at the time. He was a whiz in math! He grasped concepts quickly, and there were many days when I felt as though I could not keep up with him. When he came to me, he was already halfway through the fourth-grade math curriculum. As we started fifth-grade math, which consisted of many of the same topics as fourth grade but with decimals, I sat down to introduce him to the process of ordering decimals. He stopped me and said, "I already know how to do this." With a smile, I replied, "Okay, explain how you do this, then." He proceeded to explain the lesson to me in incredible detail. Stunned, I asked him, "How did you learn how to do this?" Without hesitation, he looked at me and

said, "I'm a swimmer, Mrs. Spackman, duh." I was blown
away. His experience in swimming and looking at time
taught him this skill at a very young age. Needless to say,
we moved on to the next lesson.

Strength in the Subject

Just as our experiences determine how much time we may need
to learn concepts, the level of interest we have in a topic can also
play a significant role. We have to be honest with ourselves and our
kids; not every bit of information they learn will be something they
like, use, or remember. The purpose of these early years in a child's
education is to expose them to a variety of concepts and skills to
open a world of possibilities for future interests and careers. You
never know what you are going to be good at until you know about it
and try it firsthand.

Tap into your child's likes and look for ways to nurture those
interests. Find books, videos, hands-on projects, and field trips that
will encourage a deeper understanding. As your child grows, these
interests will grow, but you can feel confident knowing that the
information and experiences you have given your child will continue
to aid them in all areas of their life. The more our children are able
to make connections, the better they become at problem-solving and
at viewing all learning, across multiple domains, as a connected web
of information.

Stamina

Stamina is a habit that is challenging for many. At the start of any new activity or habit, building stamina is a subconscious action in order to develop strength in a particular area or routine. Take the idea of running a marathon. This cannot be done without taking the appropriate measures to build strength and endurance. At the start of training, expecting to run several miles is not realistic, especially if you are new to this type of physical activity. Instead, you may begin with interval training and slowly increase the amount of time you are able to run to an extensive amount of time. This method of increasing one's ability is what we would think of as building stamina. Just as our bodies need to build endurance for various physical tasks, our brains always require a workout.

Help your child with developing their stamina. An easy way to begin is by breaking up tasks that can be challenging into smaller chunks of time. Let's use an example of reading. You will want to begin by determining how long your child is able to work continuously on a particular task. Once you have identified the base time frame, begin by establishing goals. Choose small time increments that you can continuously add on in order to reach the end goal. Using a bar graph to chart progress over the days provides a great visual for children. You can even encourage younger children by having them help color in the bar graph each time they are able to add more time to their duration of concentration.

Attention Span

In a world where we are constantly being entertained by television, games, and interactive toys, our attention is in a constant competitive struggle. Your child's attention span is their ability to focus on a single task without getting distracted. Depending on your child's level of concentration, the amount of time it takes to complete tasks may vary drastically. This can also vary greatly from day to day for some children. For example, Blaine would have assignments that he needed to complete at home. A strong math student, it would seem that Blaine would have no problems with completing tasks quickly, and on some occasions he would breeze through the work with no issue at all. Other days, however, we would spend what seemed like hours trying to complete problems that had taken only minutes in the days prior.

To help increase your child's attention span, you can start by introducing meditation. Before you completely dismiss this idea, know that I have utilized this tool quite a bit in my classroom over the last several years. Spending three to five minutes each day practicing being mindful effectively increases your child's ability to focus on one specific task for an extended period of time. Some other helpful tips to help increase your child's attention span include ensuring your child is hydrated. Have a refillable water bottle and encourage your child to take sips periodically. Reduce distractions that you know can be problematic, and finally, you can assist your child by asking questions to encourage thinking.

My most recent position consists of giving instruction to a combination of fourth-, fifth- and sixth-grade students. During my third year in this position, a student I struggled to connect with was in my ELA class (English and Language Arts). I had realized early on that the majority of students in my class lacked focus in reading for an extended period of time. Knowing from my observations that this was a combination of stamina and attention, I worked to develop a plan to help these students feel more successful. The first of a number of strategies that I started with involved a meditation at the start of every class. Using a simple meditation app, I had students find a comfortable spot to begin. Each day, we would start with a two- to five-minute meditation. After a few weeks, the sixth grader that I felt a lack of connection with came to me and shared that the meditations had really helped him. This young man was also in basketball and football. I asked how he thought the meditation was helping him, and he mentioned that he felt more grounded and focused. He even went so far as to his coach to have his team meditate before the start of every game.

Number of Problems

As a child, and quite honestly even as an adult sometimes, I would find myself counting the pages I had left to read. When one lacks a genuine interest in a subject area, the number of problems or length of the tasks can be daunting. Be mindful of the amount of work your child is doing at any given time. If too much is given all at once, the feeling of overwhelm and anxiousness will cause your child to freeze, unable to complete the task altogether. If your child has a large number of items to complete, sit down and work with your child to create a schedule. You may want to model how to break the tasks into chunks that offer attainable goals. Remember, these strategies must be taught. You will need to sit down and look at what needs to be accomplished. If there is only the evening to complete all the work, break the tasks into smaller chunks and assign various points in the afternoon to complete them. Set timers as reminders and be sure to work with your child in completing each of the tasks.

How Long Should Kids Be Doing Homework?

One of the questions that I get asked most often by parents is, what should my child be doing at home? My first answer, and perhaps this is the mom in me, is to allow them to be kids. I never cared deeply about my education while I was in school. I was interested and did well, but nothing would really ever *stick*. Looking back, I regret not taking the opportunity to immerse myself in truly understanding the content during my education; however, the older I got, the more I appreciated learning and understanding how things work. The skills that most benefited me growing up were not in math or reading. They were soft skills. I learned to organize, have a good work ethic, I developed my own morals, and I learned to love myself. Without these skills, learning cannot take place.

Therefore, my recommendation is to embrace the time you have with your child and allow them to be a kid. Although this goes without saying, work on developing soft skills more than anything else. When time is spent creating a foundation for learning, the odds of retaining and valuing the information are greater. If, however, you still wish to have your child work on academics, whether it be after school, on the weekends, during holiday breaks, or over the summer, I would base the amount of time on the age of the child. Above is a chart of general time frames that can be spent during after-school hours or during blocks of breaks where you choose to have learning continue. Keep in mind the saying that a little goes a long way, and in this case, it is absolutely true. Consistency has a far greater impact than the amount of time spent on a topic.

VIRTUAL/ HOMESCHOOL HOURS

Kindergarten	Third Grade	Sixth Grade
1 1/2 HOURS	2 1/2 HOURS	4 HOURS TOTAL
40 minutes - Reading lesson, practice and writing practice	40 minutes - Reading lesson, and practice	1 hour - Reading lesson, and practice
30 minutes - Math lesson and practice	20 minutes - Writing practice (including grammar)	30 minutes - Independent reading
	20 minutes - Independent reading	1 Hour - Math Lesson and practice
20 minutes - Science or Social Studies (alternate)	40 minutes - Math lesson and practice	30 minutes - Science
		30 minutes - Social Studies
	30 minutes Science or Social Studies (alternate)	30 minutes - Language/ Instrument etc.

HOMEWORK HOURS

Kindergarten	Third Grade	Sixth Grade
15 MINUTES	30 MINUTES	60 MINUTES
Alternate Days:	Base this 30 minutes on practicing new and old skills. This is separate from independent reading.	Base this 60 minutes on practicing new and old skills. This is separate from independent reading.
M, W, F - Reading/Writing		
T, H - Math		
**Alternate this weekly	Focus on areas that need practice	Focus on areas that need practice

Each night, children should be reading for at least 20 minutes or more. In kindergarten, parents are encourgaed to read with children and begin letting go of this as their child gets older.

Time frames for working at home.

Chapter 3

HELPING YOUR CHILD WITH MINDSETS

In this chapter you will:

- Understand the difference between a fixed mindset and a growth mindset

- Identify how your mindset can interfere with your child's mindset

- Identify strategies for supporting a growth mindset

A t the time of writing this book, Ian was learning how to mow the lawn. Trent and I had previous conversations to determine when we felt it would be best to start giving him greater responsibility around the house. This was the year. During his first day of learning to mow, I watched from the kitchen window as he grew more and more frustrated with starting the mower. With every pull that failed to ignite the engine, Ian would lose confidence in himself. He struggled but continued to try. During his final attempt, as his anger rose, he finally had success. A wave of relief washed over his body, and I could see his shoulders relax as a deep breath escaped him. After getting his lesson on direction and overlapping the lines of mowing, he got to work. When finished, we reviewed his work together. There were patches, and he left disappointed.

The next week, he got back to work and started again. He was still frustrated by his inability to do it all perfectly, but he persisted. After a few weeks of practicing, I saw how that young man who started with so much frustration and disappointment in his face turned into a confident and capable mower. He was proud of his work, and so were we. Now, Ian mows the lawns of two ladies in our neighborhood for a small income. His confidence in his ability to learn new skills has increased. Imagine if we had let him quit on that very first day like he wanted. If we hadn't pushed him to struggle and to continue trying even when it was difficult, he might never have realized how capable he really is.

Our mindsets can either encourage us to do great things or have us feeling defeated from the very beginning. A mindset refers to beliefs about whether qualities such as intelligence or talent are fixed or can be changeable traits. People who believe that traits are fixed think we are all born with specific abilities that cannot be altered in any way. For example, someone who says they are not good at drawing has a belief that they cannot work on the skill of drawing. What they are capable of is where they will remain. In turn, someone who has the belief that intelligence can be altered has a growth mindset. They believe that, with perseverance and grit, they are able to grow their skills with time.

Children who grow up with a fixed mindset can find it difficult to change their thinking. This becomes a habit that is instilled in their being. It will ultimately hinder their ability to learn, grow, and develop new skills. This form of thinking may then cause them to pass on opportunities and avoid challenges altogether. A child with a fixed mindset may engage less than their peers and could eventually receive lower grades. Overall, this way of thinking and believing can have lasting effects in other areas of your child's life.

Before you begin learning strategies on how to help your child with mindsets, it's important to take a moment and look at your own mindset first. Your behaviors and mindsets can directly impact the ways in which your child thinks and acts. It's natural to pick up on the mannerisms of our parents. In fact, there are probably some behaviors that you have unconsciously learned from your own parents. There have been several occasions when I realize that I have said or done something just like my own mother. If you fail to change your own behaviors, the work you put into helping your child may ultimately end up causing issues.

During my first year of teaching kindergarten in Alabama, I had a very energetic class. One boy in particular was full of life and constantly on the move. He had the sweetest little bob of hair and when he made small hops, his hair would flap up and down. In the spring of that year, I had a conference with his parents, and during the chat I commented, "I know, right!?" This is a phrase that I had learned from my aunt in Texas, and it just stuck with me. As soon as I said it, his parents looked at one another and then back at me. They started to laugh and proceeded to tell me that their son had been saying the phrase repeatedly over the past couple of months, and they had no idea where he had learned that from. Of course, we all laughed over the whole thing. I could not believe that I had such a strong impact within such a short amount of time.

When you are negative, your child is negative. When we say things, they repeat them. Behaviors are contagious, and in order for you to ensure that you are fostering a positive growth mindset with your child, a conscious decision must be made by everyone in the house to be acutely aware of what is said and how you react to difficult situations. Start by making observations on things you or others in the house may say. When you listen attentively, you'd be surprised at what you hear that you never gave any thought to before.

In order to help you reflect on your own mindset, there are three questions you can ask yourself. Feel free to jot these down on paper or even in your notes on your phone. The purpose of this is to work on identifying the areas that need to be retrained in order to help your own child succeed in life. First, ask yourself this question: how do I view learning? This idea of learning can encompass many different scenarios. Think about your opinion on schools, teachers, and the educational system in general. Your mindset on education can come from your own personal experiences or from the way you view education as it has changed over the years. Once you have your opinion on education, ask yourself why. Why do you feel this way? Our emotions are directly tied to our own mindsets. When we believe something to be too challenging, our brain sends off alerts to other parts of our body. These alerts then cause us to react without thinking. Answering these questions will help you to better understand why you react or think the way you do.

Next, ask yourself: how do I view challenges? When presented with difficult situations, are you able to stand up, or do you find yourself shying away, uncertain if you are able to rise to the occasion? Challenges give you opportunities to grow, increase your stamina, develop new skills, and explore new areas. We all react to them slightly differently. For me, I have a tendency to want to retreat and back away, but after a lot of pep talks and an immediate feeling of regret, I know that I can and will rise to the challenge. Think of some challenges you have experienced in the past. Write these down and describe how you reacted to each of them. How do you wish you had reacted? When you understand the need for change, the next time a challenge comes your way, you just might start to approach it differently.

Finally, ask yourself: am I able to adapt to change? Change can be scary for some people. The uncertainty of what lies ahead versus the comfort of where you are now can stop some dead in their tracks. Are you someone who prefers to stick to the same routine? Do you shy away from opportunities to explore and try new things? When change is inevitable, how do you feel? How do you manage to cope with what is to come? Understanding how you approach change can tell you a lot about which type of mindset you hold. Those who are prone to a growth mindset see change as an experience. They welcome new opportunities to explore and learn new things. On the contrary, those who have a fixed mindset are more hesitant toward change. This can lead to anxiety and stress. Look over your reflection and begin identifying areas where you would like to begin making changes. As you go about the day, make the effort to branch out of your comfort zone and approach new opportunities with a growth mindset.

Supporting a Growth Mindset

Understanding the importance and value of developing a growth mindset can benefit you more than you think. Our mindsets affect how we view other areas in our lives. It can leak into how you focus, the effort that is put into assignments or tasks, and the field of work that you choose to study. The reality is that, if you do not take the time to focus and nurture a growth mindset, you may be setting your child up for failure.

In my years as an educator, there has been a noticeable increase in children who demonstrate the characteristics of a fixed mindset. This belief they have about their abilities leads to anxiety, depression, and a form of learned helplessness. So much of what we do as parents is along the lines of ensuring our child is healthy, safe, and loved that we often forget to focus on their self-image and worth just as much as the rest.

By having the difficult conversations on self-image and mental health, you are able to tackle many of the early signs of developing a fixed mindset and promote healthy thought on obstacles and your child's learning processes.

It's All in How You Say Things

A positive growth mindset is all in how you phrase your thinking. When challenges become too difficult, your child may say things like "It's too hard" or "I can't do it." When phrases like these begin to surface, it's important to help your child rephrase their thinking by introducing the power of *yet*. This small word has a tremendous impact on how we view ourselves and new learning. Encourage your child to reword their thinking and say it aloud. Instead of "I can't do this," encourage them to say, "I can't do this *yet*." By including the word *yet*, their mindsets are shifting from a giving-up mindset to one that says that, with time and perseverance, they *will* be able to do it.

I attended the University of Montevallo to obtain my teaching degree. During my first year of education courses, I had a professor who seemed like the coolest person you would ever meet. She wore red stiletto heels every day. She was a bombshell blond with pink strands underneath and she was very open about her obsession with celebrity gossip. Aside from these qualities, she was always on point with her lessons. She was prepared, engaging, and informative. I would always leave her class feeling incredibly enthusiastic about the profession I was choosing to follow. There was, however, one small thing that took me the longest to get used to. At the start of the semester, this professor gave each of us a list of positive affirmations. These affirmations were short sentences that allowed us to practice positive thinking and self-empowerment. My favorite affirmation during college is one that I still use to this day: "Today I will handle any problem calmly and creatively." We were told to practice these affirmations at the start of every class. Every day, we would have to read through the affirmations and choose one that best fit us that day. We would stand up and recite the affirmation aloud to the whole class. We were all mortified at this in the beginning, but as time passed, we slowly became more mindful of the words we chose, and before we knew it, many of us were writing our own affirmations. To this day, I still have the affirmations posted in my classroom. These are a constant reminder that, with time, our thinking can change.

The more we say what we want, the more we believe in what we say. While it may seem ridiculous in the beginning, the reward for experiencing a complete shift in who you are and the role you play in this large world is important. Choose some affirmations that can help push your child outside of their comfort zone. Each year, my students and I make visual affirmation cards that we display around our room and on the tables. Phrases such as "You are worth it," "You are smart," and "You can do anything you put your mind to" litter the room as a constant reminder of their worth and abilities. You can be very simple and have a page of these phrases printed and displayed on a corkboard in their room; or you can go above and beyond and display them as larger poster-board sayings on the walls in a playroom or their bedroom. Whichever you choose, your goal is to find phrases and to encourage your child to read and recite them daily.

It may be helpful to allow your child to take periodic breaks. Feelings of frustration and overwhelm can only worsen as your child continues to work. Offer opportunities for your child to leave their work and engage in an activity that they enjoy. Time can heal all wounds, and breaks can give your child the opportunity to relax and refocus themselves to tackle the task at hand. Be mindful to not allow time to get carried away. It can be easy to get distracted. To combat this, engage in the activity with your child and then help them with rethinking the assignment or task that they are working on.

As your child struggles with challenging tasks or assignments, offer words of encouragement by reminding them that it takes time to develop new skills. Help your child relate to the idea that everyone experiences struggle by telling them of times when you have felt this way. These stories allow your child to connect to you and become able to rationalize their feelings, while also processing the fact that it is possible to overcome challenges. Your words of encouragement, listening, and support will help your child overcome their own feelings and begin to see the opportunities to succeed.

Chapter 4

COMMUNICATION IS KEY

In this chapter you will:

- Understand the importance of your mood and tone

- Reflect on the language, mood, and tone that you use with your child

- Identify effective language that can be used to encourage and communicate with your child

- Understand that perceptions of our body language, mood, tone, and words can differ

My favorite subjects to teach are reading and writing. I love to read stories. I read short stories, picture books, chapter books, and poetry; you name it, I've probably read it. That may be a bit of an exaggeration, but I am certain you get the point. Throughout the entire year of teaching various skills and concepts in our language arts class, my favorite topic to teach is about mood and tone. Understanding the way in which an author chooses to convey a scene in a book and how it then causes a reader to feel can create a deeper understanding of and appreciation for the literature. For me, this is how I am drawn into a piece of literature. With the right words, you can feel as though you are in the piece itself.

In order to teach the idea of mood and tone to my students, I use my love for fairy tales as the basis of my lesson. I have always loved Disney stories, and this makes it easy, as most of my students have seen or heard of these movies prior to this lesson. During the first part of my teaching, I will use the trailer for the movie—for example, *Tangled*—and share it with my students. I ask simple questions on what they feel about the movie, how they reacted to particular parts, and what genre they think the movie would be classified as. For those of you who are not familiar with Disney's movie *Tangled*, it's a sweet twist on the traditional story of Rapunzel. As with most Disney animated films, this is a lighthearted comedy. Once we have that conversation, I then show them a version of the movie trailer clip that has been altered. If you are interested in seeing these, I recommend looking up the "Disney *Tangled* Trailer (Horror Recut)" on YouTube. This trailer shows clips from the movie, but the way in which it is presented is vastly different and intentionally provokes the opposite emotions. Every year, kids go crazy over this lesson. It makes such a huge impact on how they view themselves as writers and on how they read stories.

The way in which you present yourself is similar to the mood and tone of a story or movie trailer. Your mood, your tone, can impact your child in terms of how they feel and what they think. So much of our interactions with our children comes from how we communicate, our levels of interest, how we word our thoughts, and the body language that we use. Each of these components work together like an equation to communicate how you feel about not only what you are talking about, but also who you are talking to. Think about your own parents—how did they make you feel as a young child? Do you think they were too harsh, or did they let you get away with practically anything? As you got older, I am certain that most of you noticed a drastic change in how your parents communicated.

My father was what I considered a very strict person. He had high expectations and wanted me to behave in a certain way. Of course, during my rebellious years, I tested those expectations. We would argue, and I would always leave feeling as though he never wanted anything to do with me. That was never the case, of course, but it was how I felt. Now, I look at my father and how he is with my younger siblings and his grandchildren and he seems to have mellowed out in more ways than I can count. His communication has changed, but deep down, I know he is the same person.

As parents, we have to find the sweet spot between coddling, being too forceful, and encouraging our children. How do we manage to show affection and yet not allow our children to run all over us? How can we show authority without feeling as though we are dictators in our homes? The answer is in balancing your communication, but also taking the time to have regular conversations with your kids. In order to find the balance, you have to become incredibly aware of how you and your child interact on a daily basis.

A large part of what I have had to learn about myself is that I can very easily throw myself into my work. I become obsessed with progressing my business, stretching my creativity, and growing in my craft. This quality can make me lose sight of those around me. I will happily isolate myself from the world in order to achieve my dreams. This, as you may have already guessed, can cause my relationships with my boys and my husband to weaken. I know that I have to consciously make a decision every week to be a part of their lives. I have to make the effort to ask questions and be interested in what they are doing. Having to make this effort does not make me a terrible mother; in fact, I believe that understanding this about myself makes me a stronger mother, because I am aware of what people and things are important in my life and I am able to make them a priority.

Communication is so much about how we use it, but also about how we interpret it. Keep in mind that how we perceive things can change drastically from one person to another. Our perceptions magnify the way in which we communicate to one another. For example, what I consider funny, another person may find rude. Understanding that perceptions play a large role in communication can be eye-opening in how we build and maintain our relationships. I had a conversation with a mother not too long ago, and she told me that her son, a student in my class, claimed that she yelled at him all the time. Knowing this mother very well, I found this to be completely false. His perception of her when she was disappointed in him was that she was yelling. A way to work around this is to be very clear in how you feel about the topic. Stay factual, and make your sentiments and thoughts known. I will tell my boys, and repeat this often, that I love them very much; however, I am not happy with their behavior at that moment. By my focusing my discontent on the behavior and not on them, they are able to have a better understanding of why I am feeling the way I am.

Have you ever thought about how many times you say the word *okay* in a conversation? I never did until I was in a professional development meeting while I still lived in Alabama. The purpose of the meeting was to discuss how we communicate to students the directions for an assignment. Before this, I would give a direction, and ask, "Okay?" to ensure that my students understood what they were supposed to do. However, if you think about how students should respond to my questions, the word *okay* has no meaning. If someone asked you "Okay?" with the inflection of a question, how would you respond? "Okay, what?" What is okay? What are they asking? Using it in a rhetorical sense would be acceptable, but not when trying to assess a level of understanding. I have to be honest; I did this a lot. After that meeting, I became hyper-aware of how often I used the word. Once this realization of how I was using the word came into focus, I found myself looking for different phrases to ensure that my students understood. I shifted to using "What questions do you have?" or "Do you understand?" I felt that I was communicating better and that my students understood the directions better before beginning an assignment.

The way to handle situations when our kids are upset or not following directions and the way to encourage them to keep trying is the same way we communicate. Arguments will happen, you will get frustrated and overreact, but it is important that we understand various strategies that will help you in correcting the situation or avoiding it altogether.

Your Words

We use words for everything. We use words to give directions, to communicate our feelings, to express our thoughts, and to interact and build relationships. Being intentional with the words that you use is important. Think about your days in an educational setting and having to write an essay—you were careful to use specific transitions and highlight key vocabulary in order to convey your thinking effectively. If words are not chosen carefully, then it can seem as though we are on a carousel, never really going anywhere with the topic. When you ask a toddler to tell you what happened today, some may begin but never seem to find an end. The famous *and then, and then, and then* phrases are spilling out after each action they take. Words are our means for communicating, but when they are not organized or descriptive enough, they can leave unsure of what is said and where to go next.

Be intentional with how you communicate your expectations with your child. Use concise and clear language. When giving directions, be descriptive, and keep your language as simple as possible. For example, if your child is engaging in a behavior you do not approve of, refrain from saying "Stop that now!" Instead, use specific words that describe the behavior you want your child to stop doing, or start doing. Saying "Please stop tapping the pencil on the table" or "Please put the pencil down and do not touch it" gives a clear expectation of what you want your child to do.

It is equally important to pay attention to the vocabulary you use. No matter the age, clarify the meaning of words. Don't be afraid to ask your child whether they understand the meaning of a particular word. Teach your child, through example, how to clarify the meanings of words and the expectations. The more we simplify and clarify what we say, the better our children will be when following through with the expectation.

Your Tone Tells All

I am notorious for talking with sarcasm in my voice. This is most likely a trait I acquired from my mother. Knowing this, I have to be mindful when I feel the sarcasm wanting to emerge in my tone, so I can keep it from revealing itself. When teaching younger children, sarcasm is not something to use on a regular basis, because it can make understanding my expectations very difficult. Yes, some students may develop sarcasm at a young age, but that cannot dictate how I communicate to my class as a whole.

Your tone, as mentioned at the start of this chapter, can affect how your child interprets what you are trying to say. It can also affect how your child feels about the relationship between the two of you. For example, if your tone often hints at frustration or annoyance, your child will most likely begin to feel as though you may not care for them very much. The same goes for when you are always questioning in your tone. The subtle "You sure?" never gives your child the confidence they need to build to be successful or independent.

Be mindful of your tone. Take a week or two and pay close attention to how you speak to your child. Does your tone reflect your mood? Does your tone reflect the time of day? The more you pay attention to these details, the easier it will be to make changes in the future. When talking with your child, use a calm tone. This is especially useful when you are feeling frustrated or annoyed at something that is happening. My go-to strategy is to use a hushed voice. Speaking slowly and quietly induces your child to calm down and listen more intently. Your helpful tone and reaction will often help your child grow even more in dealing with their own behaviors.

During one of my years of teaching, I had my students in the hallway, lined up quietly, as we waited for the remainder of the class to exit the bathroom. I have always taken pride in the way my students walk through the hallways of our school. To my mind, it is a show of respect to the other classrooms that are still in session. While lining up quietly has never been any student's favorite activity, my students (for the most part) follow the guidelines. They recognize that their behavior in the hallway reflects on our entire class. I think that is why I was so taken aback with one particular exchange with a coworker. She told me that I was far more strict with my students than she would ever be. Did my tone make her think this? Had I said something that made her believe I was too strict or harsh with students? Or could it be the behavior of my students that made her believe this to be true? My class was a great example of the fact that using a harsh tone or being too strict with one's words is not the only way to get results.

Body Language

One thing that I always tell my students, and my boys, is if my eyes are not on you when you are talking to me, then I am not listening to you. If you happen to be a teacher, then you understand where I am coming from. I will get lots of little conversations and questions throughout the day. I could be looking through papers, responding to a quick email, or working with another student, and will have a sweet cherub come to me and start holding a conversation. After various interruptions, I start to explain the importance of eye contact. Now, my students understand that, if I do not look them directly in the eyes, then my focus is on something else at the moment. I want to give them my undivided attention, because I want them to understand that they matter.

Body language combined with our tone and words help to give our child a complete picture of what we are trying to say. I like to think of all these components as a puzzle or equation; each part adds something to the final product. Think about your body language when talking with your child. Are you closed off? Do you bother sitting up and giving them your attention? Do you look your child in the eye? Help your child feel valued by getting down to their level, instead of hovering over them. The drastic difference in height can cause your child to feel intimidated by your presence.

You can also make it a point, when possible, to lean in when listening. This simple change in body language can make your child feel you care about what they are saying. Leaning forward means that you are interested in the conversation and leaving your arms at your side or open says that you want more. Pay attention to how you stand, where your shoulders are facing, and whether your body positions depict interest versus disinterest.

Finally, your facial expressions are another large factor in how we communicate. Smiling to your child as they enter the room or when they wake up in the morning can give subtle hints that you care about them. If you are like me, you may need to pay extra-close attention to your facial expressions. Occasionally, what I say may not match what is on my face.

Call a Time-Out

If there are times when frustration or stress begin to interfere with your relationship with your child, you may need to call a time-out. Sending your child to their room, or just asking for space, is a respectful way to get your emotions in check before sitting and working things out. In my home, we use the strategy a lot. When frustrated with work, or simply with what is happening at home, I will make it known that we all need a break. I will very quietly ask Blaine to go to his room. On some occasions, his emotions may cause him to fight this, but after several quiet repetitions of "Please go to your room," Blaine will reluctantly go.

We all need breaks to collect our thoughts and feelings, so don't feel bad about asking for a time-out for yourself or suggesting one for your child. Practicing this strategy early on will help your child learn how to navigate their feelings. When everyone has reached the point where a conversation can happen without getting overly upset, be sure to sit down and calmly state what you observed and what you felt. Give your child the same opportunity and come to a resolution. The stressful feelings that we experience come from the love we have for our children. The better we are able to navigate them, the deeper a connection we will have in the end.

Section II

BUILDING
INDEPENDENCE

Cooking has always been something that I wasn't very good at, unless I had a recipe. Watching others who were so in tune with the ingredients comfortably adding a pinch here and a dash there was like watching an artist carefully curating masterpieces to be enjoyed by others. For me, I struggled with the nuances and finding the perfect amounts of each ingredient. It seemed that, when I was working from instinct, food was either too salty, too bland, or just missing something.

Learning is a lot like cooking. As we grow up and gain new experiences and perspectives, the way we learn changes based on age, just as cooking adjusts based on the number of servings. Learning has to be a carefully curated masterpiece to be perfect. Keep in mind that there are also different ingredients for building independence, and they include guidance, support, information, and independence. Depending on the type of learning and the age of the learner, success depends on the amounts of each ingredient.

Let's explore each of these ingredients in order to have a better understanding as we learn to build independence in our own children. The first ingredient is guidance. Picture this as the roadmap for accomplishing tasks. Just as a map can offer you various routes, quick or scenic, you can offer various ways and methods for helping your child understand a concept or skill.

Guidance will be the way you establish the learning. What steps will your child take to learn the concept or skill being taught? Much of the time, this will be established by the teacher; however, working with children has taught me that transferring learning from school to home can be limited. This means you may need to reinforce the instruction at home to help give your child the push they need to gain momentum when working. This ingredient is pre-planned before the lesson.

The second ingredient, support, is the help you provide learners while they are working during a lesson or assignment. Think about a GPS in a car or on a phone. When the volume is on, you will be guided along the way to your destination. Reminders of when to turn to directions are offered as a support when getting to your destination.

Support will depend on several factors. The first is whether your child is learning this information for the first time or has had multiple experiences of it in the past. New information can be difficult and requires a variety of experiences and ways of looking at the information. Support will also depend on the age of your child combined with the concept of the lesson. Children who are younger, ages seven to eight, cannot reasonably learn how to multiply digits by digits. There are many prerequisite skills required before being able to accomplish this task. Finally, the amount of support depends on any learning difficulties that may prohibit your child from being successful. Understanding your child's difficulties in learning will allow you to not make excuses, but to provide the scaffold needed to accomplish the task.

Information is the next ingredient to learning. We have to be realistic. A five-year-old cannot participate in a quantum physics class. If that five-year-old can, well, it would be a first for any child that I have interacted with. The levels at which students are given information is important. Much of this is due to the developmental level that a child is in, and the rest is due to appropriate background knowledge. Take adding, for example. A child must first know their numbers and be able to identify them. Even then, kindergarteners are only expected to count up to one hundred, and only add within totals of ten to twenty. Know what information is taught at what grade level. Even then, be mindful that not every child is ready for the information presented by Common Core, and that it is important to consider the whole child and not just define them by their age.

The final ingredient to learning is independence. The way in which we instruct our kids has to change, if it has not already changed. The world has shifted from schools being the sole provider of information to a place where information is limitless. The goal of schools now is to help students understand *how* to use the power of limitless information to encourage lifelong learning, passions, and goals for the future. This means that students must work to build independence. If teachers and parents are no longer the providers of information, students must develop the independent desire and understanding of how to locate, analyze, and use the information at their fingertips.

These next four chapters will help you establish important elements of learning so that the ingredients of guidance, support, information, and independence are given in the right measures to creating a successful learning environment.

Chapter 5

Slow and Steady Wins the Race

In this chapter you will:

- Understand that children will learn at a variety of paces

- Understand that children will be stronger in some areas and may struggle in others

- Understand how life experience plays a role in a child's ability to learn

- Identify a method for providing your child with an effective learning space

- Identify the key differences between math and reading

- Understand the importance of nurturing interests as they relate to learning

As a young kid, there were two fables that resonated with me: "The Boy Who Cried Wolf" and "The Tortoise and the Hare." I often found myself reciting the lessons that I learned from these classic stories for two reasons in particular. The first was that, as a little girl, I had a tendency to stretch the truth, and it would always get me into a pickle. To be fair, I have always been a people-pleaser, and I would often tell my friends and family what I *thought* they wanted to hear. The second was that I would often rush through my work or find myself reaching a point of anxiousness, feeling I was taking too long to complete an assignment. Never could I have imagined that these two classic fables would still be lessons that I repeat on a daily basis, not just to myself, but to my students and my own boys at home.

Comparison to others is something we have all struggled with in our lives. Not only do we compare ourselves to others, but as parents, we have a tendency to compare our children to others. Part of this, and this is the case for me, is because you want to ensure that you are doing everything that you should be doing. I hear it at least once during every conference season: "Where is my child in comparison to the other kids in class?" Here is what I have learned: your child will get there. Think about the tortoise and the hare; each one had their strengths and their weaknesses. While they did not travel in the same way, they were both still able to reach the finish line.

Education means something different, and looks different, for every child. There are kids who work tirelessly with their noses in a book because they have dreams of going to Princeton and becoming an engineer. There are kids who are naturally competitive and see assignments and learning as a competition, and there are kids who struggle in one area but excel in another. No matter their path, all of these students have one thing in common: some concepts *will* be harder than others at some point in their education. Even the students who demonstrate mastery in math will at some point find a concept that will prove to be more challenging. The challenges we encounter are where the learning begins.

Think for a moment about your life as a whole. What were the experiences you had as a child? Did you go on vacations to different parts of the country or world? Were you exposed to sports or music? Did you have opportunities to immerse yourself in various hobbies or crafts? Our life experiences shape how well we grasp information. Life and learning are about making connections. These connections can only be made when we totally immerse ourselves in the joys and experiences that the world has to offer. When our brain is able to make connections between two or more concepts or experiences, the likelihood of retaining and comprehending the new skill is stronger.

I was raised by an incredibly strong, hardworking, and determined Hispanic woman. This is something that I am immensely proud of. My mother moved to the States when she was young, and my grandmother and grandfather were raised in a small pueblo in Mexico. Her experiences consisted of sacrifices and hard work, and I am happy to have gained these traits from her; however, I didn't participate in sports, go to sleepovers, or attend parties or trips that were not with my immediate family. I never considered myself a sheltered child, but I knew in more ways than one that my upbringing was different from those of the kids I attended school with. The opportunities I was raised with consisted of the beliefs and upbringing of my Hispanic family. Fast-forward thirty years into my life, and my husband introduces me to new experiences every day. I have found myself riding four-wheelers, kayaking, climbing ridiculously large rocks in Wyoming and learning about things that I had never heard of before.

Consider for a moment a little boy who is taught from a very young age to catch a bouncy ball. As this young boy gets older and has more experiences in life, he may encounter different sports that require the same skill of catching some new form of a ball. Since this young boy has had past experience with catching his bouncy ball, he is able to use what he knows and put those skills and strategies to use; however, each time he is introduced to a new sport, such as basketball, baseball, or football, he will undoubtedly have to change his strategies to fit the needs of that particular sport. His mindset and his willingness to learn have also increased because he knows that he is capable of learning this adapted skill.

Now imagine that that boy was never taught how to catch a ball as a young child. He grows up and, while in the public education system, is introduced to various sports through recess and physical education programs. This boy will most likely feel timid and less confident in his abilities due to the lack of experiences he has had. As a result, this may decrease his willingness to learn and influence him to develop a negative mindset toward sports in general.

This idea of life experiences is also true to understanding the abstract nature of various concepts. Think about where you live. Are you close to a beach? Do you have mountains near your home? Do you live in an area that experiences the seasons or do you live in a desert? Having the opportunity from a young age to see, touch, smell and hear these features increases children's understanding of abstract concepts that are taught in school. However, remove those experiences and understanding abstract concepts such as snow, mountains, and the desert can be difficult for many, especially those who are learning English as a second language.

During my third year as a kindergarten teacher, I worked to develop some hands-on experiences for my students to investigate and think critically. It was around Christmas, and we were learning all about our five senses, a favorite for so many teachers at this time of year. To help my students understand how and why our five senses are so important, I created a lesson on sounds. I took small gift bags from the dollar store and filled each of them with common items that were in my classroom. I numbered the bags and gave my students a recording sheet to track what they thought was inside each bag. They were completely enthralled with the activity. However, I took notice of a couple of things. There were two types of students who struggled with this activity, students who I knew had limited experiences and students who were learning English as a second language. The conclusion is that they lacked the information needed to make the connections.

In order for kids to have the best opportunity at understanding, retaining, and applying the information given them, we must provide them with as much information and experience as possible. When we allow students to explore using hands-on activities, experience a field trip, and develop new skills, their ability to connect learning increases. These modes, as they are called in education, encourage learning and engagement.

Scaffold Learning

Scaffolding is a very big buzzword in education. The more you understand the purpose and process of scaffolding, the more easily learning can occur at home, in more ways than one. Before you dive into the process, let's first discuss what it is. Scaffolding is a process that offers a gradual release of responsibility to students. As the teacher releases responsibility, the amount of support they give is also reduced. Take a baby, for instance. At around six to eight months, your baby starts to crawl. A natural instinct for parents is to get on all fours and *show* their child how to crawl. You may even find yourself making the rocking motion that assists all infants in propelling themselves forward. It is truly a spectacle to watch. The process that an infant goes through to learn how to walk is natural scaffolding. Before that baby is able to walk, they must learn to stand. Before they are able to stand, they must learn to crawl. This entire process that starts from birth is a prime example of scaffolding.

When thinking about supporting your child at home or introducing new concepts or skills, there are essential questions you can ask yourself. These questions will allow you to understand your child's perspective and what they need to be successful. My greatest tip is to never assume anything when it comes to what kids are and are not able to do.

What Is My Child Going to Do?

Before you get started at home, start by asking yourself what your child is going to do. This can be anything from learning a new skill to completing a task that has been supplied by a teacher or tutor. When you understand the path your child is working on, that skill or task becomes easier. Imagine having to put together a piece of furniture without any instructions. The task quickly becomes something you end up dreading.

I have a deep love for literacy instruction, which is actually quite interesting, since I never enjoyed reading as a kid.

This admiration for literacy was something that grew as I developed my craft as a teacher and found what I believed to be good teaching practices. When I entered into fourth grade during my fifth year of teaching, I found writing instruction to be incredibly challenging. I didn't have a clear image of what the final product should look like. Added to that, very few students had a genuine interest in writing stories. As I continued to develop what I believed to be good practices, I found that one special and simple thing made the greatest impact in my teaching: I started to simplify my graphic organizers. Instead of teaching students to use one graphic organizer in reading and then a separate graphic organizer in writing, I began to utilize the same graphic organizer in both content areas. Students no longer had to figure out what they were doing because they had already done it in reading. When my students realized that what they did as readers benefited them as writers, I saw a huge increase not only in success, but also in desire to write.

Be sure that you and your child have a clear understanding of what is expected and the end goal for the concept. Knowing the end goal is equally important as what your child is working to accomplish on the initial assignment. This will give you a clear picture of the steps to take for them to be successful.

What Does My Child Need to Know Already?

I mentioned that the experiences your child has had greatly impact the way they learn. In education, this is called schema or background knowledge. I mentioned in Chapter 2 how background knowledge relates to the time needed to understand new concepts and skills, but it also affects the process by which your child learns. Once you have a clear understanding of what your child is doing, you will need to ask yourself, "What does my child need to already know before being able to do this task?" For example, your fourth grader brings home some math problems to finish for homework. You look over the problems and notice that your child is working on two-by-two-digit multiplication. Thinking about what you know when it comes to multiplication, you know that your child needs to have an understanding of what it means to multiply but also needs an understanding of the process for multiplying two-by-two-digit numbers. Knowing this, you sit down and complete some review before sending your child off to work.

Background knowledge is all about pulling information your child has previously learned and being able to make connections. While it may seem frivolous to sit down and review concepts with your child to see what they know, many children struggle to bring what they learned home. It's almost as if they walk through the door and completely forget what happened that day. Have a quick discussion about what your child knows about the concept. This can be done verbally, or you can have them brainstorm a list on a piece of paper. Give a few problems or questions—you don't need many—and have your child walk you through how to answer it. Doing this warm-up will greatly benefit your child before beginning their work, as you have given them a bit of a jumpstart.

How Is My Child Going to Do It?

Our brains have different levels of difficulty in which we process and apply new information. Just like with the infant child who is learning to walk, they must complete the other stages of development first. Once you identify the *what* that your child is trying to accomplish, you have to pinpoint the *how* in which they are going to do it. How they show their learning can be grouped into six categories that fall under what education knows as Bloom's taxonomy.

This framework creates a scaffolded process in how students are able to process content and demonstrate their learning. I won't go into detail about Bloom's taxonomy, but I do want to give you a general idea of the process. For example, let's say that your child is learning about force and motion. In the beginning stages, you have to ensure that your child understands the terms force and motion. You may begin by exploring some reading material, give time to investigate hands-on and watch a few videos that demonstrate each concept. Once your child has a good understanding, you will want to build connections between the new learning that has taken place and other areas in life. Those connections, as mentioned before, help your child retain and further deepen their understanding. Finally, comes the application and creative stages. These stages require higher levels of thinking and processing information into something new. This may come in the form of your child assembling something, investigating a process, or designing a project.

Determine which stage your child is in with the concept and ensure that they have a solid foundation of lower levels of thinking before jumping into big projects. The more you are able to build a solid foundation, the longer your child will be able to withstand the storms of learning.

Differences Between Reading and Math

We often hear that some children are really good in math and others are really good in reading, but why? What makes one child good at math and not reading? Learning is viewed as learning, is it not? Well, yes and no. Other than the obvious, reading and math are incredibly different in both how we learn and how we apply that to our everyday lives. Each subject area is approached differently, although your levels of thinking do not change. We will dive into this a little more for each subject.

> During my seventh year of teaching, I had the pleasure of working with a young man in both ELA—English Language Arts—and in math. He was a student with identified learning disabilities in reading and writing, so we offered support and gave additional lessons to meet his needs. However, in math, he was a completely different learner. He thrived in math. He worked with my highest-achieving group and, while he knew he had to work extra hard to keep up with his peers, he happily accepted the challenge. His difficulties in reading and writing may have hindered his ability in math slightly, but it did not stop him from staying motivated to continue trying.

Math Is Factual

Part of the appeal of math is that there is a right answer to every problem. In fact, this is a big reason why so many teachers like to teach math; it's easy to grade and report on. While many parents are hesitant toward the way Common Core math is taught, I'd wager that the majority of teachers are seeing a positive impact from how it is teaching kids to view math. Despite what so many people believe, there are multiple ways to solve problems. Common Core teaches students how to use a variety of strategies to solve these problems.

COMMON CORE MATH

Solution #1:	Solution #2	Solution #3

$$26 + 38 =$$

$$\begin{array}{r} {}^1 26 \\ + 38 \\ \hline 64 \end{array}$$

Answer = 64

$$26 + 38 =$$
$$20 + 30 = 50$$
$$6 + 8 = 14$$
$$50 + 14 = 64$$

$$26 + 38 =$$
$$+\ 4 \quad -4$$
$$\overline{30 + 34 = 64}$$
Answer = 64

Solving simple 2 by 2 digit addition problems

Solving a simple two-by-two-digit addition problem can be approached in more than one way. Some kids may have the ability to solve addition using a standard algorithm, and others may use their existing knowledge of place value and parts to dissect the problem and solve it in their head. Each way is unique, but neither is wrong, and they both get the right answer in the end. Students, and parents for that matter, like having the ability to know they are right. It gives them immense satisfaction and encourages them to continue doing what they learned.

Remember, when working with math, the important part is that your child is able to get the correct answer and explain how they got there. Help your child make connections between previous math skills that may encourage them to view the problem in a different way, just as the example used part-part-whole to solve the simple addition problem. Making those connections will deepen their understanding and encourage them to formulate new ideas.

Reading Is Subjective

Reading, unlike its counterpart, is much more subjective in nature. Reading can be seen as an argument in many ways. There are two types of questions that can be asked in reading: literal questions and inferential questions. No matter the age of your child, they are able, to some degree, to begin working on answering both these types of questions.

Literal questions have answers that can be directly picked out from the text or illustrations. For instance, your child is reading a book about a boy who is playing with a puppy, and you ask, "What is the boy playing with?" Clearly, the illustrations show the boy playing with the puppy, but the words also state that "The boy plays with the puppy." Both of these answer the initial question, making it literal. Inferential questions use background knowledge and clues from the text to help the reader determine an answer. For instance, you may be reading about a young girl who has dropped her favorite glass ballerina and begins to sob. The author does not explicitly come out and say she is sad, but we know that, when we cry, sadness can be a reason for it. The hardest part of inferential questions is getting kids to explain why they think the answer they gave is correct.

If a student has different background knowledge and interprets the story in a different, but rational, way, they may be right in what they think. This is what will often cause kids to get so frustrated. Between the rules of grammar and the way it constantly changes, to the subjective quality of interpreting a story, kids will often get overwhelmed and frustrated. This will cause them to give up quickly.

Offer Encouragement in Different Forms

The biggest thing to remember is that not all kids enjoy school. My brother-in-law is a prime example of this. He struggled with school, and yet he now owns several successful businesses. He was able to break through the thinking that a college degree is what determines your success. Instead, he proved that a strong work ethic and willingness to think outside the box and develop new skills can open up many opportunities.

It is important to understand that not every child will enjoy school, and instead look for ways to feed their curiosity. Find what your child is good at and encourage it. Perhaps your child is good at socializing; they may become a salesman or take a lead in marketing. You may have a child who loves Legos; this could offer an opening into engineers. For Ian, his interest in dinosaurs brought us to explore geology and the opportunities for various careers in that field. We live in a world where information is at our fingertips. Use this tool as a springboard to foster your child's curiosities and explore the possibilities of learning outside the school's walls.

As a little boy, my oldest, Ian, struggled with reading. He was late to start talking and, while it should have concerned me more, I knew that he just didn't beat the drum that everyone else did. Ian would fixate on various things as a child. The first was the movie *Cars*. He loved that movie, and he would watch it for hours. He knew the words and began picking up on small details. As we walked into the store, he knew exactly which car, out of what seemed like a hundred, he did not have, based on fine details. As he got older, he started to become interested in dinosaurs. Despite his struggles with reading, he was able to read and pronounce every dinosaur name in the book. He would give endless amounts of information on each of them, often correcting me when I said things wrong. His ability to read about, comprehend, and identify these dinosaurs showed me that he was able to learn; he just needed to find something worth learning about.

Schools are beginning to identify that learning no longer comes in the form of a textbook. Instead, learning is a process of acquiring information, retaining that information, and applying it to a variety of areas in life. The more we offer these opportunities to our kids, the more they will grow and flourish.

Chapter 6

CHOOSING THE RIGHT LADDER AND GETTING BUY-IN

In this chapter you will:

- Understand the importance of goal-setting

- Identify the difference between an end goal and milestones

- Develop a plan for helping your child to set goals at home

- Understand how to provide feedback and reevaluate goals

I moved to Pennsylvania shortly after Trent and I had gotten married. We wanted to be closer to his parents, as mine were always traveling with their job. We moved to the town where he grew up, and we reconnected with his old high school friends. Janine, the wife of his high-school buddy, offered to take me to New York. I had never been, and she thought we could see all the hot spots with just a day trip. I took her up on the offer, and she was not joking. Janine took me to every monument there was to see. We used the city pass and, by the end of the trip, I was exhausted, but I felt like I had experienced New York.

The following year, my sister came in from Georgia to visit. I mentioned the trip to New York and how we could take a train for an easy day trip; however, this trip was nothing like the one I had taken with Janine. We didn't have a plan and we found ourselves meandering about with no plan or purpose. That day, we spent the majority of our time in Times Square and Central Park. We allowed ourselves to relax and enjoy the city.

Both trips were to the same location, with the same time frame, but with two totally different purposes. My first trip was meant to show me as much of the city as possible, while the second was to enjoy the smaller moments. Defining your purpose defines your path. When you do not take time to define your purpose, frustration, angst, and self-loathing begin to creep into the back of your mind.

There is a video I watched on YouTube a while back. The video is of a comedian, Michael Jr., who goes off the cuff during a live show and uses this moment to teach the importance of understanding your *why*. In the video he asks a music instructor to sing a few lines from the song "Amazing Grace." Needless to say, it was beautiful, but the second time, he asked the audience member to sing with a defined purpose by creating a scene, and the gentleman sang with so much intent and power that it brought the entire stadium to applaud him.

This video was the perfect illustration of the importance of knowing our *why*. When we know our *why*, it brings purpose and conviction to what we are doing. To do this, kids must learn to set goals. When we instill in children the ability to make their own goals and then teach them how to achieve those goals, we develop lifelong learners.

> When I told people that my kindergarteners set goals, they never believed me. The idea of a five- or six-year-old setting goals seemed a little far-fetched for most. The reality was that five-year-olds were and still are capable of setting and achieving goals. In fact, setting goals at a young age motivated them to achieve those goals. Every week, I would pull a student to my meeting area and we would assess how they were doing with their reading, math, writing and soft skills. After gathering data, we would decide on a goal. Sometimes they would have the same goal as the week before, but create new tasks, and sometimes we would celebrate and create new goals. This was a joyous time each week in my class, and they proved to me that they are capable of just about anything.

The truth of the matter is that many adults struggle with goal-setting. In fact, chances are you are just like me, in that you have probably told yourself that you were going to lose weight or start eating healthy at the start of a new year, only to fail three weeks into the month of January. Goal-setting, in my opinion, should be something we teach from a young age. The sooner we can instill this behavior, this habit, in children, the more successful and aware they become about where they need to grow.

Goals are the mechanism that helps us grow and be successful. In this case, goals are represented by a ladder. This ladder allows you to reach a location that you cannot reach alone, but you have to have the courage to step on the ladder and climb to the very top. Goals are our ambitions. They are what we wanted to achieve.

It's important to understand that there are two types of goals you can help your child build. The first goal is the end goal. This is a large, broad goal. For example, at my school, we teach our students through units of instruction. In math, they have multiple units that they work through. You can consider these almost like chapters in a textbook. It is valuable to establish big goals, but it is even more critical that you do not stop there. End goals can be too far-fetched, and thus cause you to give up and dismiss your goals altogether.

The next step to developing a realistic goal is to use your end goal to establish milestones. These are the most important of the two kinds of goals. The milestones are what will motivate and encourage your child along the way. These goals are attainable and measurable, using tasks that help you to get to your end goal. Looking at the example of a chapter in a math textbook, perhaps the large end goal is to complete the chapter by the end of the month. In order to do this, you sit down with your child and look over all the components that are needed to get it done. You and your child decide to split up the chapter into four sections. Each section will need to be completed within a week's time. These smaller goals will motivate your child to feel accomplished while also working toward the larger goal of finishing the chapter at the end of the month. We will get into more detail on how to create these goals with your child a little later in the chapter. Just know that these goals will help set your child up to succeed in all areas of life.

After establishing the milestones, it's important to identify the tasks that will help your child reach those milestones. These tasks can be projects, practice problems, watching and summarizing video, and more. The *assignments* that your child's teacher gives them are great examples of tasks that can help your child demonstrate their learning.

Before starting the process of creating goals with your child, you will want to simplify the process first. There are some key points you will want to have established before jumping in. As I mentioned earlier in this chapter, many adults struggle with creating and meeting goals. I encourage you to start small—meaning, start with one goal and work to really nurture and meet this goal. You will start to find areas that you love as well as things that you may want to change for the next goal. There is no one right way of creating and displaying goals. Everyone is different, and every goal-setting process will look different. This will help you think of all the components so that you and your child are successful.

It's Not Just about Picking the Right Ladder, It's about Getting Kids to Use It

As a teacher and a businesswoman, one of the most difficult parts of the job is getting them to buy in. Getting kids and people to care enough to have a deep desire to implement and understand the things you have to say is not easy. After all, we have no control over their motivation, their desire, or their thinking. We can only encourage and repeat ourselves until we are blue in the face. This leaves us with the question: how do we motivate our kids to reach their goals? My personal experience, as both a teacher and a mom, is to lead by example. When we are good examples of what we expect our children to do, they will begin to naturally acquire those habits.

Allow your child to be a part of the process of developing goals. It may be easier to simply create goals for them; however, the buy-in will be far less than when you get them involved in the process. Before doing this, you may want to have some ideas of goals that you would like your child to start. Remember to start small with goal-setting. Start with one goal and grow from there. Some areas to start with are reading, math, writing, social skills, or soft skills. When kids are given the opportunity to build their own goals, whether guided or not, they develop a deeper ownership of those goals, and working toward them will be very rewarding.

When I moved to Pennsylvania, I started as a fourth-grade ELA teacher. On top of learning the new curriculum, I was introduced to a concept called Responsive Classroom. After learning and developing my craft around this methodology, I cannot say enough great things about it. Responsive Classroom is an approach to teaching that believes combining academics with social-emotional learning creates an environment where students are able to learn and grow academically, socially, and emotionally. In the very beginning, however, I struggled around establishing hopes and dreams with my students. This concept is based on an idea similar to that of large end goals. Kids would often say things like, "I want to know my multiplication facts," or "I'd like to finish all the fourth-grade math units." After they were done and the precious time was spent revising, editing, and posting their goals in the classroom, they simply sat there. They were no longer goals, but more a decor item. Where I went wrong as a teacher was in not constantly revisiting the goal as the year went on. When we don't model for our kids how to go back and readjust or think about our big goals, they will simply become another item that sits gathering dust on the shelf.

Ways to Help with Setting Goals

Go big or go home; this popular saying was something I learned as a young girl living in Texas. I always wanted to do the most, be the best, and get more done. In this case, going big is not what you want to model when creating goals. Start by making them manageable. To help your child understand the feeling of success, start small and make a goal that you know can be easily achieved. To introduce a new concept like goal-setting, I like to connect it to easy-to-follow concepts before attaching it to an educational setting. Find a topic that your child is interested in—maybe your child is motivated by sports, or you want to work on building a goal at home.

On top of making the goal manageable, you will also want to ensure that the goal is attainable. In order to know if you have created a goal that is attainable, ask yourself: how will I know when my child has reached the goal? This type of goal is both realistic and doable. I often refer back to "Goldilocks and the Three Bears" for this. You want to make sure it is not too hard or too easy. Instead, look for the sweet spot. One way to do this is by reflecting on the habits and abilities your child currently has. When you are able to identify where you are right now, you will have a greater chance to develop accurate and attainable goals.

Next, you will want to find a way to display and chart your progress. Choose a location in your home that you know will be referenced quite often. In our home, we have a refrigerator station that contains a calendar, schedule, goals, and to-dos for everyone in the house. If you choose a spot that is less visited, then you are in danger of losing interest and motivation with the goals. Create a visual for charting progress, but also be very specific in how your child is making progress. The more specific you can be with children the better.

Set dates for when you and your child are able to sit down and reevaluate the goals. This can be once or twice a week. Decide on what works best for you, your child, and your family schedule. The chart that you work to create with your child will be of great importance. The more data you have, the easier it will be to evaluate the progress. Try and refrain from asking how things are going. Instead, use language that is specific. Try saying: "Your goal was to [blank]; what tasks have you done to get to it?" This will give you a great starting point, but will also give your child an opportunity to verbally tell you how they are doing.

Goal-setting has always been a priority for me in the classroom. Helping kids understand where they are in their learning and where they are trying to go gives them the opportunity to take hold of their learning and have a clear picture of what they are working toward. The more I did this with my students, the more they respected where everyone was in the learning process. It became less of a competition and more of a support system. One day, I had a mom reach out through an email (she copied the principal and assistant principal on it). She attached a picture of her daughter holding a sticky note with a list of tasks written next to bullets. The mom stated that she asked if this was her homework and her daughter replied, "No, these are just some tasks I have on my list in order to reach my goal." Her daughter then proceeded to explain to her the progression of her learning. In the email, the mom explained that she was so impressed with her daughter and how aware she had become of what she needed to accomplish and what she was working toward. After reading the email, my heart was so full of joy and happiness.

Based on the information you have, set new goals. Do not be afraid to set a goal that is easier. It is important to communicate at an early age that there will not always be successes in life. However, it is incredibly important to have a discussion on failures that does not mean that they are not good. It simply means they are learning and working. I like to tell my students and boys that the word fail is an acronym for "first attempt in learning." If you child has been successful at reaching a goal, be sure to celebrate in some way. Make a list of ways to celebrate. Keep in mind that they do not need something that costs money. Have a movie night with your child's favorite snacks, play a game they love, or allow them to have their favorite treat.

When Is Good Enough, Good Enough

Knowing when your child has met a goal can be challenging. You want to ensure that your child has retained the information, but also that they can apply their new learning to a variety of scenarios. So, when is good enough, good enough? Should a child complete a hundred problems or so many hours to show they know it? The answer is much more complex and can vary drastically between teacher, schools, and districts. My answer is that you know your child best. Base your expectations on what you believe your child is capable of doing. Just remember that answering ten problems correctly and answering fifty problems correctly are not different in percentages. If your child is able to do ten problems, then why make them do fifty?

Giving your child a variety of ways to show their learning is equally important. In math, you will want to ensure that your child can do the math through standard problems, use the strategy and apply it to word problems and finally, identify real-life situations where they may use the math. In ELA, you will want to give your child the opportunity for multiple-choice and open-ended response. If younger, the power of conversations is extremely powerful. Begin with the basic understanding of the skill or concept and help your child build it toward being more application-based.

Chapter 7

Asking the Right Questions and Giving Feedback

In this chapter you will:

- Understand the importance of asking questions

- Identify your frustrations with working on school assignments

- Identify your child's frustrations with school assignments

- Learn strategies for guiding instruction using questioning

- Learn how to give effective feedback

When I married my husband, we would take a trip to see his parents every Thanksgiving and summer. This was before we decided to move up north for good and the car rides would last us a solid thirteen hours from Alabama. During our visits, my mother-in-law would play games with us. She would pull out old games from the attic or we would have some new and exciting game to play outside. As time passed, I became obsessed with collecting various types of games or finding ways to play games during the long car rides home. A favorite of ours was always Twenty Questions. We never had to worry about packing anything and we had to use logic, concentration, and creativity.

In the game Twenty Questions, we would give the kids a topic. From that topic, we would choose an object or person. The kids would be allowed twenty questions that we would respond to with simple yes or no answers. After the twenty questions were up, they were forced to take the information they knew and guess what we were thinking. When we work with our kids at home with their schoolwork or getting them to think through a task, it is a lot like Twenty Questions in reverse. You want to guide them to understanding how and what they should be doing.

One of the biggest mistakes you can make as a parent is to pick up your child's pen and do the work for them. No doubt with good intentions, when we take the pen from our child in hopes of *showing* them how to do it correctly, there is no thinking that is taking place. Learning requires your brain to struggle and find resolution. This is when learning is able to occur.

At the height of the COVID-19 pandemic, when the world was sent into lockdown, parents were forced to become teachers. I received countless emails from parents who were frustrated, unsure how they could help their child with learning at home. Their kids were in tears and parents at their wit's end. This devastating time in our history made many realize that their child was not as prepared or equipped to learn content as they had thought.

When I married my husband, Ian was turning seven years old. He was a good boy, but, like any child, he had his challenges. Trent was thrown into an immediate father role. I could tell that he was easily frustrated when working with Ian on tasks that were too complicated for him. Other times, frustration would cause Ian to walk away crying and left Trent unsure of what went wrong. Aside from learning to take on a new role as a father, Trent struggled with his patience, phrasing, and wordy explanations. After years of discussion, practice, and feedback, Trent is home three days a week with our boys and he handles it all like a pro.

It is no secret that parents get frustrated with their children. In fact, I can assure you that your children also get frustrated with you. How we work to be proactive and prevent these frustrations is important. Equally, it is important to develop a plan for how you will also deal with times of frustration. No matter how proactive you are, there will always be times when you cannot have a plan for everything.

Frustration Sets In

When children are working through a tough assignment, there are four possible outcomes that can occur. First, the child gets frustrated, and the parent takes the pencil and begins working the problem for them. Second, the child gets frustrated and the parent gets frustrated with the child, causing the child to get even more upset and abandon the work entirely. Third, the child gets frustrated, which causes the parent to try and help, but they still end up spending an hour or more on a single assignment. Finally, the child gets frustrated and the parent guides the child through the work by asking questions and giving feedback.

Which of the four outcomes are you currently experiencing? It's okay to be a mixture. Honestly, I would be completely shocked if you didn't say that you are a mixture of all four. The key to helping your child through difficult assignments is to limit the number of times you and your child become frustrated. I cannot tell you that, if you follow all of these tips, you will never experience your child getting frustrated. I would be lying to you. I have been teaching for a decade and still have kids who shed a tear over the struggles in their learning. We are all human, and we all have emotions. What matters is limiting the number of days your child is frustrated and helping you with strategies for how to deal with a child who is frustrated in their learning.

Just like the game Twenty Questions, helping your child through their work becomes an art of concentration, logic, and creativity. Mastering this strategy may take time, but the more time you are willing to spend on perfecting this skill, the more relaxing the process of homework becomes—and you also begin to create joy and a positive experience to work on assignments at home.

Start Small

Working on any type of assignment or project can easily cause frustration and anxiety when we feel overwhelmed with the amount of work. At the start of any task, sit down with your child and talk about what the assignment is asking them to do. This may include questions such as: "What are you trying to accomplish? What is the problem asking you? What do you know about the topic/

assignment?" Depending on the number of problems or steps in a problem, you may need to break them down and start small. By eliminating the overwhelm of the number of problems, your child will already begin to feel less frustrated.

One strategy I use in the classroom is taking the paper and folding it, to only reveal a few problems at one time. When they are finished with those problems, I will check their answers and give them a break. Be careful to not allow too much time to pass; if your child gets too distracted, it may be difficult to get them back on task.

Types of Questions to Ask

In the teaching world, there are various levels to the types of questions you can ask. Think of a Jeopardy board. The questions that give you the lower amounts tend to be easier, and the larger-dollar questions are much harder. Asking your child questions should always start with the simple questions first. I consider these your literal questions. These answers can be found directly in the print. For example, if you are helping your child through a word problem, you might begin asking what they know. Once you have a good idea of where to start, you can increase the difficulty of your questions. You might ask: "What is the problem asking you to do?" or "What information do you need to solve this problem?" Be patient and strategic when asking questions.

Starting with the basic questions first will help guide you along as you determine what your child knows and what they don't understand. If you get to a point where you child is stuck, you can offer support by giving helpful hints. I often word things like this: "Think about what it is asking you the difference of" or "In the problem it says each student committed two hours a week for the nine weeks; how many weeks total did they commit to?" I do not give the entire answer, especially to multi-step problems, but I offer some guidance and opportunity to make connections.

Allow Struggle to Occur

This is probably the most difficult of all the tips in this chapter, and that is to allow your child to struggle. I mentioned in a previous chapter that struggle is when learning is possible, but it can also be the experience that feeds a fixed mindset. Finding the balance of appropriate struggle will take time. You may find that there are times when you have allowed too much struggle to take place, and other times, not enough. Determining the right amount of struggle may look different for every child and be different between assignments. For example, I know that, for Ian, reading is not his favorite. He loves to read stories and write creative stories, but the moment you ask him to respond to an assignment in a written format he will hate it; because I know this about him, I make myself available while also not hovering over him to answer all his questions.

If you know that the subject area is particularly challenging, offer support in the beginning and set yourself a time to check in with your child. Offer words of encouragement and suggestions to help your child move in the right direction. Start with five minutes, and slowly begin to add a minute until you find that your child is able to complete it all without you. Remember to be patient and embrace the awkward silence. Don't be so quick to jump in and start asking questions. On average, it is best to wait fifteen seconds before asking another question that will get them thinking.

Also, ask your child to give it their best guess. Teaching them that to try while knowing they will not get it right is better than not trying at all is a great way to allow struggle. After your child has given it their best, ask how and why they answered the problem the way they did. If you are able to make connections with what they have, great; help them see how close they really were. If your child continues to struggle, then you may need to sit down and help them through two questions. Find the balance that works for your child; just remember that the goal is to help them get to be a little more independent.

Use Resources

If you have access to various resources, or better yet, the internet, encourage your child to utilize those resources when struggling with an assignment. Begin by asking your child what questions they have or what they need to understand the problem. This may be a refresher on a skill or a term to be defined. Offer resources to help guide them through the problems.

In a world where you have an endless amount of information at your fingertips, you must teach your child how to utilize technology for learning. Keep in mind that, while your child may be accustomed to using technology for entertainment purposes, this is not the same as using technology for learning. These skills must be taught, and it is critical that you do not assume your child understands how to look up tools and resources online to assist them with their work.

Ask your child's teacher for resources as well. This can be a collection of websites, paper resources, texts, or even physical tools that can aid you in accommodating their needs at home. Keep the materials in an easy-to-access location and make your child aware of where they are and how to use them. A tool is no better than you unless you know how to use it.

Give Feedback

Information is invaluable. The information that we read in order to learn allows us to grow and achieve our dreams. Equally important is the information that we receive as feedback. This information is indispensable. Our perceptions of our own abilities and talents can be very different from what others perceive. Feedback allows us to take in multiple accounts and viewpoints to ensure that we are achieving at our very best. In many cases, getting feedback is the most critical part of the learning process.

While you may agree that giving your child feedback is important, the ways you provide that feedback is essential. The manner in which we talk, how we offer our opinions and insight, and how we guide our children to make corrections can be a sensitive topic. Understanding appropriate strategies for giving feedback will prepare you for having conversations with your child regarding their work, but will also support you in encouraging your child to make adjustments in order to be successful.

Be Specific

Growing up, I remember how my heart would sink to the pit of my stomach as my teacher returned graded assignments. On each paper, I would find simple phrases with large scores circled in a vibrant red. Each paper would read some version of: "Good work," "Well done," "Keep trying," or "You need to study." I would either be overjoyed that I did well or be completely perplexed with what I did wrong. The power of specific feedback encourages children to dig deeper into their understanding of the concept and look for misconceptions.

When giving feedback, use language that gives specific examples. It's not enough to say, "Great job!" Find examples that help tell your child what was great. If your child is working on a writing assignment, then find areas where you feel the child excelled; by going even further and telling your child why these were great, the likelihood of their repeating this in the future is greater. The same goes when giving your child feedback to make improvements. You want to be specific and tell them what they did wrong. Take a child who is working on subtracting multiple-digit numbers. You notice that your child is not borrowing from the next place value, making the answer incorrect. When giving feedback, you will want to express your observations in a clear and factual manner.

Give a Glow and Grow

A great strategy that is widely used in business when conducting performance reviews is to give feedback beginning with a positive comment, followed by a growth point, and concluding with another positive observation. The theory behind this approach is to start the conversation in a nonconfrontational way. This will reduce any stress on the individual receiving feedback and opens the flow of communication. Once a dialogue has started, it becomes easier to offer potential for growth.

Children respond best when following this same approach. To make the verbiage more kid-friendly, one widespread popular method is to call a positive a *glow*, and to call a negative a *grow*. Each time you review your child's work, offer a glow and a grow. The glow will encourage your child to continue the behavior and the grow will provide your child with specific feedback to analyze and correct.

Model How to Improve

When you take the time to give feedback to your child, you will also want to ensure that your child understands how to begin making the corrections immediately. Model how to correctly complete the task using an example problem or question. After you have shown your child the correct method for solving, have your child try to use the new learning to make the appropriate corrections. I recommend watching over the first two to three problems and offering guiding questions and immediate feedback. This approach will scaffold your child so that they feel confident in their abilities while also ensuring that they are completing the tasks correctly.

Practice and Repeat

As with any new skill that your child is learning, practice is a key component to ensuring that retention of that skill is maintained. Offer opportunities throughout your child's learning experience to continue practice of various skills. Multiplication facts are a great example of a common skill that needs consistent and continual practice to maintain. As children enter into more difficult math, reciting multiplication facts will allow students to confidently complete more difficult math easily. The saying "Use it or lose it" is accurate in many cases when learning new content. If multiplication facts are not consistently used, children will find math more challenging to complete without a calculator.

Every child will reach a point in learning where frustration begins to set in. Encourage your child to persevere through challenging tasks by offering guidance with questioning and feedback. If you are like me and have a child who is nearing more complicated skills, then utilize the internet as a resource. Asking your child questions to guide them through research and learning is a powerful experience and skill to acquire. My favorite phrase to use as a teacher is a simple "Show me." These two little words remind me that it is the child who needs to explain and show how to complete the task, not I. As you continue to aid your child through their learning process, remind yourself that it is up to them to learn and process the information. Consider yourself a trip guide and your child the traveler, taking in every piece of information to interpret the greater meaning of it all. Your job is to help them take notice of all the smaller details.

Chapter 8

PUT YOUR KIDS TO WORK!

In this chapter you will:

- Understand the value that work such as chores and responsibilities has for your child's education

- Understand the impact that chores and responsibilities have on your child's self-esteem

- Identify strategies to encourage responsibilities at home and school

- Determine whether you will offer payment for responsibilities

My mother-in-law enjoys making pottery. Her creativity and joy in this art form allows her to create unique pieces that she sells at local antique shops. Her hobby has provided my boys and I an opportunity to learn a new skill in this art form. We have explored various types of clays, tried our hand at spinning bowls, and made unique and creative pieces that we now proudly display in our homes. Each time we came over to Kelli, my mother-in-law's, house, we would spend a few hours listening to music and making new pieces of art.

After some time, Kelli decided to place the boys' art up for sale for a small price. We created signs and small price tags indicating that the specific art pieces were made by a six-year-old. Her hope was always to encourage them to create more and understand the value of earning money. One day, after coming home from work, Blaine was so excited that he could barely contain himself. Apparently, during one of Kelli's visits to the location where she sold her art, the owner gave her a letter and over twenty dollars in profit. The letter was written by a woman who came into the shop and was completely enamored by the fact that Blaine was creating pottery to sell.

The letter shared the lady's excitement over his art and said that she wanted to continue encouraging him to make a new piece. She had purchased two pieces that day and, for what would have cost her barely a dollar, she gave twenty. That day, we read that letter over a dozen times. Each time Blaine would flush red, and you could tell he was just bursting with pride. He went back to work ready to begin selling again.

Pottery is an art that requires a tremendous amount of time to complete. Over the course of several weeks, Blaine would mold his clay, allow it to air-dry, and apply his glaze. His patience and dedication through a process that can last several weeks had paid off.

His confidence was boosted and his excitement over creating was greater than ever before.

While having your child be responsible for jobs around the house may not seem as though it ties in with excelling in their education, I would argue that it has a role in ensuring your child is successful in school and outside of the classroom. Part of education that is beginning to make a large shift is building connections between learning in the classroom and the real world—developing skills that involve money or digging deeper into the science and understanding of force and motion. These skills can easily be taught through the concepts of saving money and spending to work smarter, not harder. It helps answer the age-old question "Why do I need to know this?"

The responsibilities and jobs we give our kids at home also instill essential soft skills that are required when learning. Examples of these soft skills could be communication, organization, collaboration, project management, and attention to detail. Building an incredible work ethic outside of learning will encourage children to use these skills when in school or completing assignments outside of school. We forget that, as our children get older, they still need to be taught new skills. Teaching these skills will allow kids to learn them in a familiar environment. When we compile too many skills, whether academic or soft, your child will become easily overwhelmed and frustrated.

Soft skills were a big priority when building our multi-age team. We understood the direction education would, and should, be headed. When we presented the structures of the team to our principal, we incorporated various soft skills that we would encourage our students to learn. During our first big project, we spent countless lessons helping kids organize, hold discussions with peers, and organize information to help them come to new conclusions. We encouraged collaborative disagreements by helping kids understand how to listen and disagree with one another, and we spent a lot of our time getting children to appreciate and respect everyone's journey. We knew that learning how to solve a particular kind of math problem or learning about the process of growing plants could be found online. What we focused on were the skills needed to help kids continue learning even when they left school.

This may seem hard to believe, but there was a period in my life when I had no idea what I wanted to do. I transferred to Coppell High School in Dallas, Texas, in the middle of my sophomore year. Those remaining years of high school were really hard for me. I had no idea who I was, and I felt so out of place. I struggled with learning, and I was on the set path to barely even graduate. I remember my vice principal sitting down with my parents, trying to see how they could get me to graduate with the minimum number of credits required. College didn't work out much better. We moved back to Houston when I graduated, and I attended Jefferson State Community College. At that time, I had no clue what I wanted for a career path. I jumped from psychology to interior design to business in less than a year. I failed every class and, with the most regret, didn't even take the time to drop the class. I accepted the zeros. Learning just wasn't in my cards. I took about two years off from school and worked various jobs. I was a waitress for Red Lobster. I became a culinary manager at the age of nineteen and moved to Alabama in the process. I had a tremendous work ethic, but little academic knowledge or understanding of how the world around me ran. I was street-smart. My learning would start when I turned twenty-two. Thankfully, I had acquired so many soft skills through my various experiences that I felt confident knowing that I was able to learn anything I wanted.

Having set jobs also creates a feeling of value and appreciation. Children feel rewarded at the completion of a chore, and they know that their accomplishments have in some way made you happy. Children, especially at those younger ages, want to please their parents and their teachers. Your satisfaction with them helps encourage them to continue working and developing those essential life skills.

Find a Job to Fit the Age

Start giving your child opportunities to contribute to the family at a young age. For most families, parents will start by having their child pick up toys around the house or their room. Develop personal responsibilities such as cleaning up their toys, putting away their clothes and vacuuming their rooms. As your child continues to grow, the jobs can become more frequent, and intensive. However, you do want to be careful not to assign too many chores all at once. Too many chores too soon will set your child up for failure. This entire process should be scaffolded, just as when they are learning something new. Start small with easy-to-manage responsibilities and grow from these as your child demonstrates they are able to handle more.

It is much easier to add on responsibility than it is to take responsibility away. Imagine your own boss sitting down with you and telling you they are taking away one of your responsibilities. This is similar to a demotion. Questions begin to emerge: "Why? What did I do wrong? Am I not good enough?" These insecurities are threatening to your self-worth. Now, imagine your boss telling you they have decided to increase your workload due to your amazing job performance. The feelings from this circumstance are ones that add to your self-worth. Children experience these exact same feelings.

Therefore, it is important to help set your child up for success and the feelings that accompany success by scaffolding their responsibilities and continuing to add to them as they show levels of competency.

Give Praise and Feedback

In the previous chapter, we discussed the importance of feedback. Supporting your child through the process of completing jobs cannot be done without the proper encouragement and feedback. In the beginning of giving my own boys new jobs around the house, I use the same scaffolding techniques that I use in my classroom. This ensures that they have a clear understanding of what is expected of them.

Before starting the job, I will model for them what I expect. It may seem weird at first, but as you are showing your child the correct process, talk out loud about what you are thinking and doing as you do it. Then, have your child tell you what you did and what was observed. Here, you can give clarification and remodel if you have to. During your child's first time doing the task, stand over them and give praise and feedback. This is a critical part in your child's learning and in your child's confidence. Follow the glow and grow format that was discussed in Chapter 7. Be mindful that you are giving equal amounts of praise and feedback. This will limit frustrations for both you and your child.

Every weekend we have a list of household chores that we want the boys to finish. On our refrigerator, we have a small whiteboard that allows us to keep track of each boy's list. As Blaine has gotten older and is learning to write, he works hard each weekend to write out his own list. One of the items that is always on his list is washing the windows. We have two large glass doors that are filthy because of our dog Walter, so we have given Blaine the task of cleaning it on Sundays. The first time he was given the task, he watched as I cleaned the porch door. When it was his turn, he sprayed and wiped and sprayed and wiped. Each time, I would give him a few pointers. When it came to cleaning the very top, I told him to think about what would help reach all the way up. He whined and grumbled, but after some time, he walked over with a stool that we kept in the kitchen. When I high-fived him and told him it was smart thinking, he beamed with pride. Weeks later, Blaine has become a glass-washing pro.

Equally, be mindful not to take the task over to *show* your child how to do it correctly. This can be challenging, as the urge to just do it yourself to get it done faster and right is the typical impulse. Your child will not do everything correctly, and your child will not do everything quickly. The learning process takes time, but it is important to allow your child to grow at their own pace. If needed, you may have to give yourself permission to walk away. This will give you a break to ease the frustration of wanting to complete the task yourself, but it will also reduce the stress that your child may be feeling. It can be nerve-wracking learning a new skill. Your child is probably nervous that they might do something wrong or that they will not be good at the task. Ease your child's mind and remind them that this is a learning process.

To Pay or Not to Pay

Growing up, I was given an allowance. This had nothing to do
with the chores; this was just something that my mother and father
started to do because they wanted me to learn how to manage money.
It was great for me. I was able to buy things I wanted—at that age,
I was really into comic books and movies. Of course, my mom and
dad always took care of the essentials; the allowance I had was to go
toward the extras. I knew that, every week, I could depend on that
allowance, no matter what.

Trent and I have taken a different approach. Even though we both
experienced allowances growing up, we wanted to teach our boys
what it meant to earn money. We wanted them to understand the
value of working hard, being rewarded for that job, and then learning
to save money. After a lot of discussion and tweaking over the
year, we ended up deciding that there are certain jobs around the
house that are family responsibilities. These are jobs that they do as
contributing members to the family. They do not get compensated,
but they get appreciation from other family members. Some
examples other than maintaining their rooms and their belongings
are to empty the dishwasher, clean the windows, take out the trash,
vacuum the rugs, and dust the house. Both Blaine and Ian have a
set chore list, and every year, after their birthday, Trent and I will sit
down and reconsider their list. We may add on or move one chore to
the other child. It truly just depends.

There are other ways our boys can earn money. One way is to work
on various art projects and offer those for sale, like Blaine's clay
pieces. A second way is for them to find jobs in the community; for
example, Ian mows two lawns and, as we transition to winter, he
will offer to rake and shovel snow. Finally, we offer our boys various
opportunities to earn money at home or at my in-laws' farm. For
example, on our refrigerator, we have small hook magnets where we

can place a small index card with a chore written on it and money clipped together. We will then hang the clipped money and chore on the fridge from a binder clip. At any point during the week, either boy can offer to do the job and earn the attached money. These jobs can vary from scrubbing down the shed doors, to doing some extra weeding, to cleaning out the garage or cars.

Some weeks, they are incredibly motivated, and other weeks, they are not. The reason we love this method so much is that it instills in their brains that they must work in order to earn money. They understand that their parents are not money machines and will not buy them everything they want; I also like that they don't have a constant desire for more *stuff*. We live in a society that is constantly wanting the next best thing, and overbuying is a real issue. We try to teach our boys that stuff does not bring joy; experiencing new things in life and appreciating the world around you can offer you so much more than having various material items.

We also decided that we were going to teach our boys to save. Blaine does not earn enough to start saving, but when the time is right for him, we will do the same as we do for Ian. When Ian earns any type of money, he knows that he has to save 80 percent of his earnings. It does seem like a lot, but he has plenty left over to purchase small items here and there. He has now opened a savings account and is accumulating a decent amount of money that will help support him as he gets older and begins to make a life for himself.

Deciding when and how to start teaching your child to manage money is very personal and is something that you should discuss with your partner. You may decide to simply offer an allowance each week, or you may choose to go the route that Trent and I have decided on. Whatever you decide, be sure to take the time to sit down with your child and explain the process and responsibility of earning money. Help with deciding where to store money, the responsibilities that money brings, and most importantly, how to count money. I say that last part jokingly, but it is such a great skill for kids to learn.

As with everything else that we have discussed in this book and will continue to discuss, a conscious effort has to be made on your part to ensure that your child is maintaining everything. Have a set day and time to sit down and go over their chores for the week. This is a time that I like to call Quality Check. Give feedback using the glow and grow model, and set a specific amount of time for them to complete the tasks. This is important. Setting the time frame for them to make corrections adds pressure, but it also gives you the ability to set it to your schedule. This will reinforce them to make it right the first time instead of constantly having to redo it at their own pace.

Section III

RESOURCES TO SUPPORT

I f you were to look through your kitchen cabinets and drawers, you'd find a variety of tools that you may have collected over the years. Perhaps you went through a baking phase after watching *Cupcake Wars* on The Food Channel, or maybe you were watching an infomercial and purchased a new Ninja Foodie. Whatever the case may be, the kitchen is one of the easiest places where you can accumulate so many pieces of equipment.

Having a variety of tools in the kitchen can help you make your cooking routine more efficient and consistent. Take the KitchenAid mixer, for example; there are so many options for various attachments. You would most likely start with a simple mixer, but you could expand to the pasta maker, the vegetable strainer, the sheet cutter for making lasagna, or my personal favorite, the slicer/shredder attachment. Each of these tasks could be done with a simple cutting board and knife, but the process would be more labor-intensive and take longer.

Within the field of education there are a ton of resources, tools, and supplies that you can use to aid your child in learning. While the intention of these items is to benefit you and your child, they can ultimately make learning more difficult and overwhelming. Learning is a process that has been happening for years without fancy materials. Yes, technology is advancing, and your child does need to learn how to use technology, but it is important to develop those core foundational skills, such as soft skills and goal-setting, first, before introducing new and more difficult elements. The marketing industry fools us into believing that we have to have every resource and new technology to help encourage our children to learn at home. I am here to tell you that you don't.

I have always had a love for planning. I would acquire a ton of notebooks, colored pens, stickers, and various organizational tools. The more items I accumulated, the more organized I felt.

The older I got, the more elaborate my planning materials became. I found myself with four different planners at one point in my life, each one served a different purpose. As my life became more complicated, with children, jobs, business, grad school, and now this book, I quickly realized how inefficiently the multiple planners were. I condensed my materials and found that my life went from complicated to simple.

As children learn new skills and concepts, their brains are processing a lot of different bits of information. The more we change their learning experience and add on new tools, the more difficult it can be for them to process the information we want them to learn. For example, take learning how to compare and contrast a topic. As a teacher, there are so many different ways I can have my students compare and contrast a topic, but most often we start with using graphic organizers. This helps kids to organize the information in a logical format; however, there are a variety of compare-and-contrast organizers out there. What I have found from my research and practice is that changing the graphic organizer can take away from the learning that I want to occur. Remember, the focus is on the comparing and contrasting the topic. The moment I change the graphic organizer, the attention refocuses to "How do I use this graphic organizer?"

While you may look at it from the viewpoint of trying to engage your child with something new and exciting, too many resources and changes in how they learn can feel overwhelming and misconstrue the learning that should be occurring. In the beginning, stick to a few essential resources. Build the essential skills and foundation using what you have, and, as your child becomes more advanced and capable of processing multiple pieces of information, add on the complexity.

This is a time to be creative with your child's learning. No, you do not have to be a creative person, but more an outside-of-the-box thinker. Learning can happen in the most inconvenient and odd places. Take advantage of what you do have and build real experiences that encourage conversation, inquiry, and exploration. The world we live in is an opportunity for learning and, when we view our experiences as learning, we build our own educational platforms.

In the chapters to follow, we will discuss a variety of resources that will help you encourage learning and manage it. You will explore establishing a learning space with your child, create routines and schedules that are conducive to your child's needs, learn how to assist your child with learning key organizational skills, and finally, you will learn strategies on holding your child accountable. These final chapters will help you to take everything that you have learned and begin putting it into practice in an effective but also realistic manner.

Chapter 9

BUILDING A SPACE THAT ENCOURAGES LEARNING

In this chapter you will:

- Understand the importance of creating a workspace in your home

- Answer essential questions to help in identifying the best workspace

- Identify the best workspace for your child in your home

- Identify resources that encourage your child to learn

When children go to school, they know they're going to learn and work. From the backpacks that fill with learning materials, to the clothing they put on, each thing signals to their brains that they have to work. As they arrive at school, their bodies go through the motions of routines. The environment they experience in school is one that limits distraction and creates a space of learning. A classroom is free from most distractions. Children quickly learn the expectations and therefore know their purpose during those six to seven hours.

As kids transition to the home, their distractions begin to increase while their level of concentration decreases. Our homes hold a variety of purposes. We spend time with family, we cook, we eat, and we relax after a stressful day. For most, coming home is a signal to our brains that we are ready to wind down and relax. Children struggle with the transition from school while needing to complete homework. When they get home, they want to relax and decompress from the day of information overload.

Helping your child establish a space that allows them to focus on their work is important. There are very few children who are capable of establishing a functional space that will allow them to focus and get work done. As a parent, you want to help build that space for them. Teach them how to maintain their space, how to use the space, and how to adapt it to fit their learning needs.

The space you help your child create also needs to work for your home and the needs of your family. If you are like me, your home may not offer a lot of places where your child can work away from distractions. Taking into account the size of your home, the number of individuals sharing the space, and finally whether the space needs to be multifunctional is important. The hardest part of establishing a workspace is defining it to work for the various needs and sticking to it.

As your child gets older and their learning becomes more complex, this skill of establishing a workspace will become more critical. Your goal is to help your child identify what is going to work best for their needs and their style of learning. Once that space has been defined, the most essential component is training your child's brain to use it for work.

Think about the times when you've wanted to start a new routine or learn a new skill. For me, it's always working out. Having the right equipment, the space laid out, and the workout clothes does absolutely nothing for me unless I make the effort to actually do it. I will often tell my students that learning is a two-way relationship. I can give them the information, support them through the journey, and supply the tools, but if they do not choose to engage in the lesson, ask questions when they are stuck, think through the process, or make the effort, they will leave the same as they were when they entered my classroom.

Questions to Ask When Defining Your Space

I love designing spaces, decorating, and making a space feel cozy and relaxing. I will often joke with people that the reason I became a teacher was because it contained everything I wanted to be in one. I get to learn about the brain and why we react in different ways, I get to create a classroom space that is relaxing and inspires, and I get to sell information to my students using essential business and marketing skills. Of course, with any profession, there are a few essential steps and questions that you need to ask yourself before diving in.

If you are like me, creating a learning space for your child is probably the priority. I look to Pinterest and my favorite design shows to get inspiration for how to structure small spaces; however, it is incredibly important to remember to get your child involved in creating this space. It needs to be something that works for your child and that they feel excited about; after all, your child will be the one who is using the newly created workspace. With some guidance, you and your child will be able to create a space that works for the both of you, but before you jump in and begin planning out your child's space, you have to answer three essential questions.

Does Your Child Get Distracted by Sound?

Sound can either help your child focus or it can cause your child to be distracted and frustrated. Sound is an element you really have to consider when establishing a space for your child to work. Think about the sound of traffic, meaning, are people going to be walking in and out of the space? Consider sound that travels from one area of the house to the other. We live in a small home, and our living room and dining room are attached. This means that, if there is someone on the couch watching TV, then the person in the dining room may get easily distracted.

Consider the times of day when your child will be using the space. My husband works from home and, if it is summertime, I cannot work downstairs at all. There is a lot of movement and devices that are playing. If you or others in the house are going to be working or coming home to relax, you may need to negotiate times when devices are on and when it is quiet and time to work. You may need to try out a few areas of your house to see what works and what doesn't. Have frequent conversations with your child about how well they can focus when there is noise and determine together what works best.

Does Your Child Need to Be Away from the TV and Items that May Entice Them?

We've established that our homes can be the breeding ground for various distractions throughout the day. This makes establishing an effective learning space a little trickier. The television in a home can be incredibly tempting, especially if your family likes to keep it running in the background. Video games, toys, and computers are also items that can draw your child's attention. Of course, this may not be an issue for every child, but it is important to consider. Blaine does not often play in his room by himself, but if he had to do work in his room, I can guarantee he would start to play rather than complete his work.

If you have the ability to tuck items away, such as in baskets that hide toys, or a console that tucks away, you may be better off than you think. However, if you have lots of items that are in plain view and that limit the ability to reduce distractions, you can either find a new location in your home or find simple solutions to minimize the distraction. Begin by finding locations in the house that will allow your child to focus on the task at hand. Once you've decided on a few locations, then you may need to have a family meeting and come to a compromise. I personally like to have the TV off until after dinner. This allows me to have conversations with my boys while it encourages them to get homework done, and it gives me time to decompress from the day at work. When everyone is able to get on the same page, then we contribute to each other's success.

Does Your Child Need to Be Someplace where They Can Be Held Accountable?

Children need accountability. There are very few children who are able to hold themselves accountable to complete their learning at home. When deciding on a space, you need to consider how often you need check in on your child. This will look very different for every child, and if you have multiple children, you may have different standards for each of them. Find what works best for your child, but more importantly for you (unlike the other two questions, which are focused on the needs of your child). While the demand for accountability is still on the child, this process will require more effort on your part. Therefore, if you feel you need to hold your child accountable more often, find a location where you can do frequent check-ins.

The great thing about this question is that you can have multiple areas in your home. For Ian, we allow him to work in the basement. However, with routine check-ins on his grades twice a week, if he has demonstrated that he is unable to maintain his grades, he knows he will have to move upstairs to the dining room. You have the control when deciding the answer to this question, but it is a great idea to build in the accountability and reward by scaffolding your child to a different area as they prove they are capable of maintaining their work and focus.

Finding the Right Space

Everyone's space will look drastically different. Depending on the area you have available and the number of people who will be sharing the space, you may need to be creative. The key to finding the right space is not how luxurious it is or that your child has their own desk;

it is all about consistency. The focus is to get your child trained so that, when they sit down at this space, they will be getting ready to work. The more regular you are about getting them to use the space, and the more consistent you are with the times when they must be there, the easier it will be to get your child focused.

In the very beginning of finding the right space, you may need to make adjustments. My boys do not have desks in their rooms. I mentioned that we have a very small home, and it simply is not feasible for us to give them their own desks. However, we have plenty of surfaces they can work on. So when we first started deciding where each of them was going to complete his school assignments, we had to come together and decide as a family what would work best. Most of the time, Ian works downstairs in the basement, and Blaine works upstairs, with Trent in our studio/office. In the beginning, we had both boys working in the dining room while we either worked on the couch or in the kitchen. As everyone adjusted, we were able to make different choices.

Maintain consistency for an extended period of time. Try to stay away from making drastic changes quickly. You may think, during the first week, that the space is not working, but it could just be an adjustment period. It will take some time and reminders, on your part, to get kids in the rhythm. During the first few weeks of school, a teacher will spend the majority of the day practicing routines and procedures over and over. After some time, maybe two to three weeks, then you may want to sit down and decide whether you need to make some adjustments.

There are those very special and rare occasions when it is so much fun to change things up. These are times when you notice that your child is working especially hard, and you decide to make things a little more fun by shaking up their learning location for the day. Blaine has two kinds of schoolwork. He has paper and pencil items that he has to complete, and then there are a few activities that he has to complete on his Chromebook. During those special days when we know Blaine has been working hard and is able to focus, we treat him by allowing him to take his Chromebook to the bed or couch to finish up his assignments. During those rare treat times, he is reenergized and so excited.

No learning space can be functional without the right materials. If the locations you end up choosing are like ours, where there is little storage and no real desk space, I encourage you to create a learning box. This can be a simple basket, a Sterilite container, or a bag that can be tucked away in a closet. Inside this learning box are all the materials your child might need when working on their assignments. In our family we use a simple basket that we purchased at Target. It has handles on either side which are perfect for Blaine to carry on his own.

Inside this basket, we keep a folder of paper, a cup filled with colored pencils, a dry-erase board and marker, and a bag filled with items to use when counting or working on math. Before he sits down, which has recently been at the small desk in our studio, he will grab his backpack and learning box. He takes out all of his materials and is able to get to work without scouring the house looking for the right materials. This reduces distraction and gives his brain another signal to begin working immediately. Creating a learning box will also make it easier to move locations at a moment's notice.

Using Resources to Understand Learning Outcomes

Besides finding the right location for learning, other than the couch or bed, finding the right tools to help your child learn can be frustrating. I am here to remind you to keep it simple. Even though technology is developing at an increasing rate, you have to remember to establish foundational skills first. Thinking that technology will solve your problems and help your child learn is wrong. Research has shown that, while children are considered digital natives, meaning they are able to operate and feel very comfortable with technology, they do not understand how to use technology as a tool for learning. They see technology as an entertainment device.

In my first year teaching fourth grade, I entered a district that was heavy on technology. Each student was given an iPad to use during the year. Fourth grade was the first year that students were allowed to take the devices home. As I handed them their iPad and charging cable, it was as if they had just received the MVP award. They were over-the-moon excited. Of course, we had many conversations about the responsibility that comes with having an iPad and proper safety rules to use online. During my fall conferences with parents, I remember the parents of a certain kiddo in my class coming in with worried expressions on their faces. Partway through the conversation, they asked about his behavior with the iPad in school. I remembered having to redirect this kiddo from time to time, but there was nothing I found really concerning. They then proceeded to tell me that they would prefer that the iPad stay at school, as it was causing issues at home. During one weekend, they had caught him in the attic, sneaking the iPad to play games in the middle of the night. Of course I agreed, and the iPad never went home unless there was an assignment due the next day.

Technology is a blessing for so many, but it is not the be-all and end-all. In fact, many of the resources you would buy in fancy learning stores are not needed. I once took a trip with a company called BBT Edventures, where I worked as a leader to guide other teachers to a different part of the world, give professional development sessions, and explore the school systems. This trip was to Jamaica, and during it, on our final day in the schools, I had the immense pleasure of speaking with a young man in a third-grade class. He very proudly showed me his math toolkit. It was a simple shoebox that he had covered and decorated, and inside he had various tools that he used when working on his math assignments. Every item in the box was something he had created using paper, colored pencils, markers, cardboard, and glue. During the teaching of each new concept, they would create new tools to add to their boxes. Shapes that were cut out and labeled were pasted to cardboard for durability. I was blown away by this level of creativity. Think of the pride he had and the knowledge he gained while making those tools. Creating items can be much more powerful than simply picking up a store-bought product.

There are also opportunities to use items in your home for learning. The measurements when cooking in the kitchen, the sizes of various tools in a garage, and the opportunities to count all the various objects can create a fun and exciting learning space for any child. During those early years of learning, reading, writing, and math can be easily taught using everyday tasks. Encourage your child to write out the grocery list to practice spelling and numbers. Label furniture and objects in the house or go on a number walk and look for items you can count. If you need to give your child a visual for math, you can use dry pasta, whipped cream on a cookie sheet, or magnets on the refrigerator to give them hands-on practice.

As they get older and the skills become more complicated, you may need to use technology to aid you both. There are a ton of resources out there to guide you and your child. Take advantage of this time and use it as an opportunity to research. Look up definitions to unknown words; find examples online. I always push my students and my boys to find more than one source that says the same thing. This increases reliability and helps make sure they understand the task at hand. Many times, my students will ask me how to spell a word, the meaning of a word in reading, or how to solve a problem, and my answer will be to look it up. When we have the power of a device and a wealth of knowledge at our fingertips, we have to make sure we are teaching our kids how to use it properly.

You simply don't have to have all the fancy equipment, the shelves lined with books, or the grandest workspace ever. The reality is that so many simply do not have that luxury. It is very possible to work with what you have. Be creative, think outside the box, and most importantly, teach your child how to use what is available to achieve the desired result.

Chapter 10

Establish Schedules and Routines

In this chapter you will:

- Understand the difference between a schedule and a routine

- Create a schedule that is reasonable and sustainable for your child

- Develop routines that your child will be able to consistently and successfully maintain

D riving the same route every day becomes a routine that you could do with your eyes closed. Obviously, you don't want to drive with your eyes closed, but there have been many occasions when it felt as though I had. I would drive to school and not remember a single detail of how I had gotten there. Routines and schedules are like your drive to and from work. On the days when you are able to hit every green light, you know that your day will go smoothly. However, on those days when you've hit every red light, gotten stuck in construction, or have seemed to hit traffic, it is a hint that you'd be better off just going back home and calling in sick.

Your routines and schedules help you manage your time and affect your moods. Just like an infant who didn't get their afternoon nap, a minor setback can send you into in tears and make you cranky for the next few hours. The routine and schedule you establish may be dictated to you, or it can be something you create; no matter which, it is the lifeline to ensuring that you are able to get the job done within the expected time frame.

We have already established that children like to have routines. It creates a sense of comfort and allows your child to know what is happening next. It also prevents you from hearing a broken record throughout the day. Think of this as being like a bell schedule in middle or high school. As the bell rings, each student collects their things and shifts to a new topic. We all have routines, yet creating and maintaining them at home can be a bit more challenging.

Our home lives can change at the drop of a hat. One moment you can be following a routine and, in an instant, you might have neighbors come over, or you might even get sucked into Netflix, binge-watching a new series that was just released. When you are in the comfort of your home, it is three times as hard to stick to your schedule. It becomes easy to make excuses and tell yourself you can do it later. The same goes for our children. They will often make excuses or, sadly, may even tell you they have finished the assignment when in fact they have not.

Before getting started on establishing a schedule with your child, it is important to understand and help your child distinguish the difference between a schedule and a routine. Use the terms, even at a young age, to help your child develop these essential life skills. A schedule is an outline that designates particular sets of time to spend working on a specific task or a block of tasks. To help your child understand more clearly, describe the blocks within a classroom. There is a chunk of time designated for ELA, math, lunch, specials, and recess. During each time block, students work on assignments they are assigned to learn and grow in for that area. Your child will have one schedule that may be adapted as they grow and need to work on various skills or concepts; however, for the majority of the year, your child will most likely adhere to the schedule you create in the beginning.

With regard to routines, however, you and your child will create several, one for each area in their day. A routine is a set of strategic tasks that your child will work to help them during specific blocks of time. A routine does not have a strict time block, but can be viewed as the steps taken when working in an area. For example, when students come into my classroom during reading, they will begin by taking out their books and reading independently for a set amount of time. Afterward, they will engage in a lesson that lasts for about fifteen to twenty minutes and will work on the strategy at their tables. As they finish their independent work, students will start work on goals we have set together. Every day the routine is the same. On the rare occasion when we are celebrating author's day, or I want to throw in a fun day, we will veer off track. The routine that you build with your child will ensure that all the tasks get done and eliminate guesswork.

Now the question arises: why do you need both? Some may believe that, by establishing a routine, you are creating a schedule. However, a routine does not have the time guidelines that a schedule does, and the argument may then be that they are given each step in a routine a specific time frame that needs to be adhered to. The response to that is, how does it not then become a schedule entirely?

Many people already take the time to build a schedule and routine for themselves and for their children; the hardest part of this entire process is following through with the schedule and routine that you have created. Accountability is the largest component to ensuring the success of an effective schedule and routine. No matter how well you are able to think out your schedule, no matter how creative you are with posting it in your home, the schedule cannot force you to use it. It will take accountability, choice, and willpower to ensure that your child is following the schedule every day. Understand that you will make some mistakes and need to make adjustments, but the overall goal is to try to stick to the schedule and routine to the point where it becomes second nature.

I am a checklist girl. I always have been. In fact, I have even been guilty of writing a checklist and listing all the items that I had already completed just for the pure satisfaction of marking it off. When I became a teacher, I quickly realized that there are a lot of moving parts to what happens in a classroom. From making sure I was on schedule, to lunch, to making sure I had prepped everything before my students walked in, I needed a quick solution. I decided to start making a morning routine and afternoon routine checklist. For the first week, I kept this checklist on a notepad. As I did my routine each morning, I would write down the items that I did and update it as I went through the week. By the end of the week, I had a solid checklist that I was able to use. I found that, by creating his checklist, I was able to make sure all the items that needed to be done were ready to go each day, but it also helped me in other ways. First, I found that, on days when I was really thrown off my routine, my checklist was my lifeline. I knew that, even if I was feeling overwhelmed or scattered, I could open up my checklist, take a deep breath, and start marking things off. Second, when I wasn't able to be in my classroom, my checklist helped keep things going. I could have a teacher friend, or a sub, just pick it up and make sure that all was running as it should.

Creating a routine and schedule should help you feel less stressed and more in control of what your child's day should look like. It will decrease the anxiety in your child and, after some time, reduce the arguing that takes place about whether your child should do their work. Your child will come to know what to expect and, as you remain consistent, it will become second nature.

Creating a Schedule That Works

There is no perfect way to create a schedule that works without trial and error. As with so many things in life, there will be times when you have to make adjustments because you've forgotten something or realize that you've given too much time to one area of your life and not enough to another. Life is a balancing act that requires constant attention and management. Begin by looking at what your schedule looks like now. Depending on the times when you are working, times when your child is engaging in extracurriculars, and those nonnegotiable family times, you may only have a limited time frame that you can work with. Creating a schedule will be like the game of Tetris; finding spots to encourage learning is important. Even if your child does not have homework, use the time to have conversations about where they are in their learning. This can be a fluid time that helps blend what is happening at school and at home.

Most children struggle to see the connections between school and home. For my boys, they leave school, and they want to leave everything else with it, even what they learned. However, our goal as parents is to encourage conversation and help our kids see the relevance of what they are learning in school to the real world. Blocking off time in your child's day to work on homework or talk about what is happening in school is one step toward making meaningful connections and holding your child accountable.

When creating a schedule with your child, there are a few factors you may want to consider. Our lives are like seasons that are ever-changing; children have extracurricular activities, church, or family responsibilities. As you look to establish a schedule, keep in mind all of the activities your child is involved with. Begin by blocking off items that are nonnegotiable. For example, let's say that you know from November to January your child is in wrestling. This means they will participate in practice Tuesday and Thursday evenings from six to seven in the evening. Most Saturdays will be spent in competitions, and in January, you may have several weekends when you are completely booked. Other seasons may be a little more low-key and allow for a lot more flexibility. Balance the amount of work your child is doing with the amount of extracurriculars.

My husband is adamant about our boys being involved in sports. When I was a child, I was never forced to participate and get involved. I was in chorus and played the flute for a few years, but that passion faded as I moved to Dallas during my sophomore year. For me, extracurriculars were something we could choose to do but were never forced. When Trent told me that we would be taking the approach his parents took, I did not counter it. In high school, Trent was given two options: You can play a sport, or you can get a job. Trent decided he would join a sport during each season. For our own boys, they have the same options. Blaine is active in sports as he decides what he is interested in, and Ian spends his time on chorus and mowing lawns. This keeps their schedules busy, but not so busy that it takes up all of their time.

Use blocks as a way to chunk out your child's day. This approach to scheduling is more realistic and can offer you a general idea of how much your child has on their schedule. When you start to get too detailed by planning with smaller increments, it can easily get overwhelming. These types of schedules can also leave room for tasks to leak over into other times, which can result in unfinished tasks. The scheduled blocks give you a general idea. For example, if you are at home with your preschooler, you may have from nine to ten in the morning as their time for soft play. This time frame allows for you to give your child enough room to explore a variety of soft play materials, but it also gives room for times when you find you are running a bit behind schedule.

Schedule in breaks. These can vary from ten to twenty minutes of unscheduled free choice. They give your child a necessary break from more structured tasks and allow their brains to relax. With breaks, you'll find your child has more ability to refocus and get back on track. Be sure to keep these relatively short. My preference is for ten to no more than twenty-five minutes. Times that are longer than this can cause issues with getting their attention back on the task at hand.

Finally, consider your child's attention span when scheduling times. Children, and most adults, have very short attention spans. Teachers will often keep their new, direct instruction under fifteen minutes, as children are known to begin losing focus on the lesson after that. From my experience, children are able to spend one and a half times the direct instruction time working independently. Asking your child to complete fifty math problems in one sitting may be too much for them. Let's take Blaine's schedule as an example. My son has three types of tasks that he needs to complete. He needs to read aloud, write up to four sentences, and finally complete a few math problems. Each of these activities should take no more than forty-five minutes to an hour. That's roughly fifteen minutes for each task. Within this time, I may offer small breaks, so in his schedule he has an hour and a half blocked off to complete his schoolwork once I get home. This gives him plenty of time to work and take a couple of breaks if needed. If Blaine completes his tasks early, he is given free time, which he loves.

Ian, on the other hand, has tasks that take more time and concentration. On average, Ian has two to four homework assignments that he needs to complete every day. His assignments may take, on average, twenty-five to thirty minutes each to complete. I will block off around two hours for his schedule when he comes home. This will give him time to make a snack, unpack, and get to work at the table. One strategy that I teach the boys when working on an assignment is to circle problems they are struggling with and move on. At the end of the assignment, I will look over their work and help them with any problems that they circled. This keeps their momentum going, keeps their mindset positive, and keeps their schedules on track. For any assignment that I feel they are really struggling with and leaking too much time from their schedule, I will either write a note on the assignment that they need more help and instruction because it was too hard or send an email to the teacher asking for another day. Homework assignments should not take up your entire evening.

Create a Routine

Once you have a schedule that you feel confident will work for you and your child's needs, the next step is to develop a routine for that block of time. Children can easily become creatures of habit with consistency and perseverance. Work with your child to develop a routine that they feel confident they can complete and sustain. Think of all the finer details, from where they will put their belongings to where they will sit down and with what materials. As you decide every bit of your child's routine with them, walk the path and time it. You will want to ensure that the routine is not so extensive that it takes up the entire block.

Agree on the steps your child will want to include, for example, snack. My boys love snacks, and it's important for us to have a variety of snacks available that won't take too long to make and can get them right to work. There are two areas where our boys can grab snacks. The first is in the center drawer of the refrigerator, and the other is a snack basket in the pantry. This lets them know what is available without having to search for food. You may also decide where your child will be during certain time blocks. If you are detailed in this routine, you find that what we discuss in the final chapter, along with everything else in this book, will be easier to sustain.

Above all, keep things simple. Try to avoid dictating their every move. That is why creating the routine together is helpful. Have your child walk you through what they think would work, and, during each step, ask questions and offer suggestions that work for the whole family. This is something they will have to do, and, if you simply tell your child how to do it, the likelihood of it going well in the beginning is small. Finally, I have said it before, and I will say it again: it's easier to add things on than to take them away. Start small with the routine, and, as you realize your child is successful at the tasks, you can add things on later. Once you and your child agree on the routine, create a visual. If your child is younger, take images of your child doing the routine and print them out. Post them in order in a visible place. If you have an older child, simply write it out, but keep it visible. Quick tip from a teacher: there are small portable laminating machines that are phenomenal. If you laminate your child's list, you can use a dry-erase marker to cross items off. Kids enjoy the satisfaction of crossing off items as they work. Setting your child up for success now will help them in the future.

Chapter 11

TEACHING ORGANIZATION

In this chapter you will:

- Understand the importance of organization to your child's learning

- Identify various areas to help your child get organized

- Learn strategies that will help your child become better at organizing he scariest time of the year for me as a mom and teacher is the end of the school year. Kids are charged with the task of cleaning out their desks, cubbies, lockers, and materials. Only, when this happens, some students will simply pile everything into their backpacks without even looking at it. Ian is very much this child for me. The dreaded end-of-the-year backpack comes home, and it feels as though I'm in an action movie, charged with trying to defuse a bomb. Every year I find the most interesting, and disgusting, items in their backpacks. One year, I remember throwing out the entire backpack as it *just wasn't worth saving.*

Teaching children how to organize is, in my opinion, one of the greatest factors contributing to your child's academic success. Organization is a soft skill that translates into organizing materials, ideas, information, schedules, and routines. These everyday tasks that we use as adults are beneficial to start learning at a young age, because as your child gets older, it may be more difficult to replace current habits. This chapter and Chapter 8 work really well together. Much of what was discussed in Chapter 8 will help encourage your child to organize more often.

The goal for this chapter is to help you see the connection between physical organization and your child's success, beyond the obvious aid in locating homework. I will share some stories of my own organizational journey with my students and my two boys at home. Hopefully, as I give ideas and some of my own examples, you will feel inspired to start helping your child make adjustments to what they are currently doing. Remember, start slowly. Revamping every single thing, while tempting, may not be as successful as you think. Work with small pieces rather than giving your child an entire chicken breast to scarf down. As your child is able to consistently and correctly organize one area, then strategically add on until you find your child is able to handle multiple components at once.

As I write this book, this is the first year I have had to have desks in my classroom. Individual desks for each learner, the kind with the opening right below the writing surface for kids to store their supplies. In the past, I have always used tables. I liked the collaborative atmosphere that tables encouraged, and it always seemed easier to have kids clean up after themselves. Luckily, we don't have textbooks and other large-format materials that students need to maintain this year, and I like to take a very minimal approach to learning tools, as I have found a few pieces that I think are most valuable to have all the time. Plus, I am incredibly fortunate that my district is one-to-one. Each student receives an iPad to use for the year as a learning tool. This keeps me from using paper that can easily get lost or damaged. However, only a few weeks into the school year, I was making a cup of coffee in the back of my room. I glanced toward the front, giving each child's desk a quick look, and noticed that papers, wrappers, and other materials unknown to me were protruding from the holes in their desks. I walked over to get a closer look and was astonished by where these materials had come from. I decided to have my students empty their desks that morning. Now, well into the school year, we will clean out our desks once a month to ensure that materials that should be going home *are* going home.

Organization can impact every part of our lives. The obvious aspect of this is organizing our materials. It can be easy to accumulate an overwhelming amount of stuff. This can lead to frustration, anxiety, and in some difficult cases, disorders. Developing early organizational skills is something we start at a very young age without even knowing it. Think about a child taking their shoes off. They may either choose to leave them where they are, which, it can be argued, is a form of organization, or they may put them in a closet.

Logical organization is something we start to do on our own, mostly because we see our parents doing these tasks.

As we get older, however, organization becomes more difficult. Part of this is due to how much we accumulate, but it also occurs as we begin to add other elements to our lives. For instance, as your child starts school and sports, there are items you will need to organize for school as well as for their sport. Each area will need some structure as to where things belong. This is also true as their areas begin to expand. When your child goes to school, they will have a space there, along with other materials that they will need to be responsible for. Developing strategies and skills in organizing early on will continue to benefit them as they progress in life.

Organization can also impact the tasks that we perform in a day. These tasks, known to your child as to-dos, assignments, or chores, are important for them to develop an organizational system to manage their growing responsibilities. In Chapter 10, we touched on scheduling and routines as a method of organization, but I will share some other ideas and strategies to help your child with the transition from school to home, and vice versa. Remembering to complete assignments, ensuring you have all the materials you need, and managing your child's responsibilities at home can be overwhelming as you work to manage your own busy schedule, along with those of any other children you may have.

Working to develop strategies at home on time management and organizing tasks effectively will aid your child as they begin to have multiple tasks coming in from various parts of their lives. Think of a middle or high school student. Their school day consists of multiple teachers who give them projects, assignments, or to-dos. Combine this with having to organize tasks from their extracurriculars, home life, and relationships with friends, and it can be quite challenging, to say the least.

Ideas are the final area of our lives that must be organized and maintained. So much of what we do in a day consists of problem-solving, projects, and multi-step situations that require us to think about how to organize the task itself. Organizing an idea can be challenging, as it requires you to process the information, translate it, and organize it in a manner that makes sense for you. Take a household problem, for example. You go to use your blow dryer in the bathroom, but it doesn't work. Without thinking, you try to reset it by pressing the red and yellow buttons on the plug. Nothing works. Your brain is organizing the problem into steps you are taking to solve the issue.

Children will begin to learn how to organize information at a very young age. Graphs and models are the earliest ways that children will organize information. As they begin to work on more complicated tasks, they will need to use what they understand about organization in a concrete sense and apply it to more abstract thinking.

Organizing Materials

For some, organization means having a home or workspace that is neat and tidy. As you walk into the space, there is little to no clutter on the surfaces, and everything is tucked away from sight. This idea of organization is not necessarily universal. Organizing materials, put simply, is making arrangements of the materials into a structured whole. Your home may not be the neatest, but neatness has nothing to do with organization.

When I think of organizing materials, my first thought is finding each item a home base in my household. This does two things: first, it gives me a place to put the items when they are not in use; second, it ensures that I can find the materials when they are needed. When considering what home base you and your child are going to use for various items, think of locations that make logical sense. Get your child involved in the process. Ask questions like "Where do we want our soccer shoes to have their home? Why do you think it would be best to put them in the garage?" These types of questions will offer your child the opportunity to develop an understanding of how to organize, but they will also help them remember the location they chose.

Once you have determined a home base for the item, then decide on the system in which you want those materials to be placed. This will look drastically different for every collection of materials you and your child organize. If your child has a number of materials they need to use for assignments, then decide on how you want those materials organized. Find a box or a pouch to hold pencils, glue, and scissors. Use a folder or canister to keep loose paper or construction paper in one place. Whatever you choose, discuss the importance of keeping the materials organized.

Create labels to finalize how the items will be stored. The labels will remind your child what you both agreed on. If you're anything like me, you may not like having a ton of labels because of aesthetics. Trust me, I get it. The good thing is that you can choose to make semi-permanent labels that you can take down once the habit has been formed. If your child is still too young to read, then take images of the object, or of your child holding the object, and use those as labels instead. I would still encourage you to use the picture with a label to help your child begin to relate the word to the object. This is an easy form of reading.

As you find places for materials and decide how to organize those materials, make the conscious decision to keep them in one place. My husband will often joke that I am notorious for moving things around, making this especially difficult for him and the boys; and while this is very true of my personality, I have also had to make the decision to maintain the organizational method that I started with. This helps everyone in the household know exactly where things should stay. If you find yourself getting frustrated because the location or system is not working, give it a few days before deciding to move things around. If you do decide to make some changes, be sure to make everyone in the house aware and give it time in the beginning.

It may also be beneficial to minimize the number of items and locations where things are kept in your home. We have been on a decluttering journey for a few years now, and I am amazed at how little I miss all the extra things around our home. Work to keep things fairly minimal by looking for items that are extras or serve no purpose. If you find, after a couple of months, that you or your child has not used a particular item, consider getting rid of it.

Organizing Tasks

Scheduling and routines play a huge role in time management, but it is also important to teach kids how to manage a variety of tasks. What good does it do to have a block schedule for your child's homework if they cannot remember their homework in the first place? Children can develop this through their school assignments, the chores they are responsible for at home, and any extracurriculars they have. Organizing tasks helps your child know what they need to do.

In upper elementary school, teaching kids to organize their tasks for the day is incredibly important. Unfinished work and falling behind on assignments are not uncommon. So it was incredibly important to find a solution to help kids manage their time and their tasks wisely. After immersing myself in a variety of organization and time management books, I decided to teach my students how to create a power list. Each day, they would come into my math class and sit down. The very first thing we would do was to create a list of three items they wanted to accomplish. As they worked to finish those items on their list, they would cross them off. If, at the end of the day, there were undone items on their list, then those items became homework. This was a simple and effective way to get students to learn to manage their time and tasks and know what they needed to complete for homework.

Help your child find a way to organize their tasks. If you find they're forgetting items at school, then talk with their teacher about incorporating an agenda in your child's day. My school doesn't offer our students agendas, but I have gladly worked with parents in the past to allow home agendas and ensure that their child is completing them. To verify that what the child wrote was correct, I would initial the agenda at the end of each class day. If needed, ask your child's teacher if this is something they can do. I have asked Ian's teachers to do this in the past and it has helped him tremendously in remembering his homework assignments.

When you have a list of tasks your child needs to complete, whether chores they need to work on at home or school/extracurricular assignments, then you need to help them decide how these tasks fit into their schedule. It can be easy to feel overwhelmed and get frustrated with a large amount of work. As I discussed in Chapter 2, work with your child to chunk the tasks into a more manageable workload. This may mean that you need to find two tasks your child can complete within a specific amount of time. Once those tasks are done, then offer your child a break and find more tasks that they can work on. This will not only make all their tasks more manageable, but it also helps keep your child accountable, something we will discuss in detail in the last chapter.

Organizing Ideas

This final organization method may be the most challenging of them all. However, with discussion, patience, and connections between the idea of physical organization and this, more abstract method of organizing, your child will benefit greatly from the practice. Math problems are a great example of a time when children will need to organize their thinking. Multi-step word problems are becoming more critical for students to be able to solve. These problems, as the name implies, consist of multiple steps that need to be taken to find the solution. Students must be able to process the information and think of the steps required in a logical and sequential format. The same goes for teaching your child how to organize a story they are writing into a sequential and coherent writing exercise. Start by asking simple questions, such as "What do you already know?" You can offer more guidance by asking questions where the answer is clearly stated. For example, if the math problem clearly states that Bob has 306 stickers, then ask your child "How many stickers does Bob have?" Then lead them to think about what needs to happen first. Keep in mind that you will want to offer a break for them to complete each step between questions. If you try to talk through the entire process, your child may feel overwhelmed and easily forget what they needed to complete first.

> One of my favorite activities in kindergarten was to give my students a cup of buttons that I had collected over the years and organize them into groups. I was always so fascinated by their methods of organization. Some kids would organize them by color, number of holes, if it had a ridge, or by size. We would have discussions about why they decided to organize these buttons as they did and compare our methods. This was proof that kindergarteners were capable of organizing objects using logic and creativity.

Help your child work through their ideas by asking questions to guide them through the process. Use colors or images that give students a visual to tie to the thinking. For example, when I had my kindergarteners tell a story, I would have a green, yellow, and red card in front of them. As they told the story, they would point to each color. This would help them gather their thoughts and remember them later. I especially like using color highlighters when teaching kids how to organize their thinking. We will use various colors for word problems, editing our writing, and finding information in stories. This takes a very boring idea and gives it a little more depth with the colors.

Remember that this is a challenging skill. Be patient and take your time helping kids organize ideas. You'll find creative and simple methods that will keep them on track and support them in their learning and success at home.

Chapter 12

HOLDING YOUR CHILD ACCOUNTABLE

In this chapter you will:

- Understand the importance of accountability

- Recognize that the first steps to accountability lies with you

- Develop logical consequences for holding your child accountable

D o you remember ever working on a project in school that you were crazy passionate about? For me, it was my fourth-grade class in Houston. We were studying Egypt, and I vividly remember each student creating a large 3-D replica of an Egyptian pyramid. I wanted to learn everything possible about Egypt, and I poured my heart and soul into creating my pyramid. I was so proud the day I walked in with it. I remember the shocked faces, the gasps from peers, and the comments from friends.

Now imagine that very same project. Days pass, weeks pass, and you realize that the project you spent hours working on never receives an ounce of recognition from your teacher. You are gutted. Your passion begins to fade, and soon you wonder why you even bothered in the first place. If this happened to you, would you even give thought to completing any future projects for that teacher? The answer is most likely no. Accountability is what drives us to sticking to habits, competing tasks, and furthering ourselves in our passions.

As you work to help your child succeed in all areas of life, you will quickly find that accountability is the key element that will contribute to their success. Children must learn to have accountability within themselves, accountability for their actions, and accountability to those who work with them. Everything we have discussed in this book means nothing if there is no accountability.

I tell people that I am a jack of all trades. I love to learn new skills, be creative, and stretch my abilities to the limits. This means that I have a terrible habit of putting too many to-dos on my plate at once. Since I spend so much time devoting myself to my job and various passions, I have little time to engage in a healthy exercise routine. It's no secret that health and exercise are my least favorite topics, and therefore the area of my life that I focus on the least. One summer, a very dear friend of mine convinced me to spend time walking each day while chatting on the phone. In the beginning, I hated walking, but loved the conversation. As time passed and we continued this routine, I started to look forward to our walks. Slowly, my endurance grew, and I found myself going on my walk even if my friend was not able to talk that day. She was my accountability buddy. Her consistency and encouragement got me to the point where I was able to go on a walk and enjoy it.

Accountability plays two major roles in your child's life. The first is whether your child is able to take accountability for his/her actions. We all know that mistakes are going to happen. Failures exist so that we can experience success. However, when times are hard, and mistakes do happen, will your child be able to say it was their fault? Owning up to behaviors and actions can be difficult for any child.

One part of my job, that some people may not recognize, is putting out little fires throughout the day. Arguments happen, actions are taken, and before any learning can occur, I may have to address what is happening. At the beginning of the year, I speak a lot about choice. This is a word that is near and dear to my heart. In fact, I have it in very large letters in the front of my classroom as a constant reminder. We discuss how we will all make choices we regret; we will make careless choices, bad choices, and choices that seem like a great idea but don't always work out. What I want kids to understand is that we also have a second choice that lingers ever so closely to our mistakes, and that is the choice to fix it, to own up to it, and to accept the consequences of it.

In my years of getting kids to take accountability as a teacher, I have realized that there are three things that encourage this. The first is listening. Listen to your child without judgement or scolding. They have a reason for their actions or lack thereof, and it is important that you try to see their point of view. The second is understanding. Help your child understand the consequences. Help your child understand how it may affect others, and, most importantly, help your child understand that mistakes happen. Finally, give kids time. Kids need time to process, to think, to make themselves believe that everything will work out. Accountability is scary for kids, especially when it is something they want to take back. Our job is not to judge them, criticize them, or condemn them. Our job is to help them correct those mistakes.

Every parent wants to have a child who is accountable, not only for their mistakes, but also for ensuring that their responsibilities are being upheld in the first place. To achieve this, I have found that two major steps need to occur. The first is that accountability begins with the parent. Children need a model for what self-accountability looks like. This means you need to hold yourself accountable for the responsibilities you have in the home, and outside of your home. My mother and father were this example for me, just as I work to be the same for my two boys. Going back to my Egypt project at the beginning of this chapter, if my teacher had not held herself accountable by giving feedback and grades, I might never have completed a project again, or at the least not to the same quality level. Accountability leads by example.

Define logical consequences in your household and stick to them. Hold yourself accountable to hold your children accountable. To see change, you must take the first step. To create these logical consequences, have a discussion about the problem with your child. Discuss how this affects others and how it will impact their future. Help your child see these connections. Most of the time, children act in the moment or fail to see how it can come back to haunt them in the future. When giving consequences, my go-to strategy is to ask what they believe the consequence should be. Kids are smart; they know what will happen and can communicate this very well. This takes the pressure off you administering punishment, and instead leads them to view it as something that happened because they didn't hold themselves accountable. Finally, be consistent and stick to it each time. You have to make the choice to sit down and have these discussions with your child. Sending them to their room without understanding why and how to make corrections will only create tension. Communication remains the key to establishing accountability.

The second step is to offer your child assistance with accountability. We talked about scaffolding as the process of slowly weaning your child toward independence. This is no different. Help your child by setting up checkpoints for a project or throughout a specific time frame. You may check more often in the beginning, with full intentions of weaning to establish independence over a specified period of time. Decide in advance how often you will check in with your child. Set a reminder on a calendar and give it a specific time. For example, I check Ian's grades on Wednesday, while my husband checks in on Fridays. If he shows us that he is able to maintain his work and responsibilities, then we may remove the Wednesday date. Over time, the goal is to only check in during progress reports. This takes time, and you may find that one child is able to grasp the concept quite easily while the other does not. Learning and growth do not happen at the same rate nor at the same time. Be mindful that every child is different and will need different experiences and support.

Our Hopes and Dreams

During my years learning about Responsive Classroom, a training for connecting academic success to social-emotional learning, one way we built a classroom community and culture was by establishing rules together. To begin, we asked what our students' hopes and dreams were. What do you want to accomplish this year? What do you want to do? Once we all had an opportunity to share and make our hopes and dreams visual, through art and writing, we built the rules to accomplish those dreams. We each knew that the reason for the rules was not because I had made them rules; rather, it was to help each student in my class accomplish their hopes and dreams for this school year. They had built the culture and community that would make each student feel and be successful.

Parents want nothing more than to raise a healthy, respectful, hardworking, and kind individual. This is our hope and dream. Every day I sit back and think about the opportunities I want for my boys, the experiences I want them to have, and the friendships and love I want them to share. To do this, to give our children this chance in life, we have to raise thinkers. We have to raise children who are willing to lead by example because they learned from example. While I cannot physically do this for you, my hope and dream is that this book has offered some guidance and clarity on how you can make your own hopes and dreams a reality.

Understand that we are all at different points in our lives, and while we may wish that life was a linear path, it curves, has dead ends, and takes you to unknown places. Embrace the journey with your child and encourage them through their successes and failures. Know that your child's path may look different from everyone else's path, but it is *their* path, nonetheless.

Acknowledgments

I used to think that my success in life lay with my ability to work hard and focus on what was important to me. What I didn't realize is how much I relied on those around me in order to succeed. There are so many people in my life that have contributed in either small or big ways to where I am today. The saying: *It takes a village* could not be more true in this case. While I cannot begin to express my gratitude to every person that has impacted my life, I want all who know me to understand that I have nothing but the greatest appreciation for them.

First and foremost, I want to thank my amazing and supportive husband, Trent. You have, without complaint, supported me through all my ambitions in life. You have endured times of frustration, defeat, and self-doubt. It is clear that all of my successes are really *our* successes; without your ability to keep our household going, none of this would have been possible. You are truly my rock, muse, and champion. Thank you for all the love you give, even when it is undeserved. I look forward to many years at your side, and I am beyond lucky to have you as my husband.

To my beautiful boys, Ian and Blaine. You have taught me so much about being a mom and a teacher. Your passion to explore new things around you reminds me of the importance that period in your life has on who you will later become. It is because of the two of you that I push myself to be better.

This goes without saying, but thank you to my dad and mom, Nomi and Maria Yusafi. You raised me to value the importance of hard work and commitment. You both have shown me, through your own sacrifices, that my success and path in life lies with a strong foundation in my morals and responsibilities. You both have given so much to everyone around you, and I could not be more proud to have you as my parents. Thank you for your support, love, and confidence to succeed. I love you more than you know.

To my incredible in-laws, Kelli and Dan, you both have been a tremendous support system throughout this process. Almost eight years ago you welcomed me into your family with open arms. Your experiences and unique perspectives opened a world very different than anything I have ever experienced. Thank you for your continuous love and support, and I am so very appreciative and lucky to have you both in my life.

To my amazing friend, Michelle Emerson, you have pushed me to be better in more ways than you can imagine. You have been there when I've needed to vent and when I needed a shoulder to cry on. You know better than anyone else the struggles that we go through on a daily basis as teachers and entrepreneurs. Thank you for your guidance, encouragement, and understanding. You are an amazing individual, and I only wish you knew the impact that you have made on my life.

Finally, I would like to thank everyone in my Central York family. From my administration to the teachers that I have the privilege to work with every single day, you all have supported and helped me to grow as a professional and educator. Central York has allowed me to flourish as a teacher and push myself to be better. I am very lucky to have landed in a district that values its educators and trusts the decisions that we make in order to better the classroom experience for our learners.

About the Author

Bridget Spackman, a public-school educator, has worked on developing curriculum, instruction, and assessment for her district in the areas of social studies and English language arts. Bridget established the first multiage program in her district and provided instruction to over seventy-five learners each year across multiple grade levels. Bridget focuses her research on providing authentic learning experiences that lead to building twenty-first century skills that will encourage and benefit her students for years to come.

While continuing her efforts as an educator, Bridget also works to inspire and provide strategies to educators around the world. Through her presence on social media and YouTube, Bridget discusses methods of literacy instruction that provide authentic, relatable, and attainable instruction to students and powerful tools to building autonomy, independence, and motivation. She also writes curriculum across various grade levels that enable teachers to easily implement her teachings into any classroom setting.

Bridget Spackman lives in Central Pennsylvania with her husband, Trent, and two sons, Ian and Blaine, along with their goldendoodle, Walter. As a mother and an educator, Bridget was afforded the unique position to see both the tech driven/STEAM-led learning abilities of Ian and the kinesthetic/active interaction of Blaine. Given the vastly different learning preferences residing under her own roof, she understands the necessity and the importance of implementing adaptive learning techniques in her classroom.

Mango Publishing, established in 2014, publishes an eclectic list of books by diverse authors—both new and established voices—on topics ranging from business, personal growth, women's empowerment, LGBTQ studies, health, and spirituality to history, popular culture, time management, decluttering, lifestyle, mental wellness, aging, and sustainable living. We were recently named 2019 *and* 2020's #1 fastest growing independent publisher by *Publishers Weekly*. Our success is driven by our main goal, which is to publish high quality books that will entertain readers as well as make a positive difference in their lives.

Our readers are our most important resource; we value your input, suggestions, and ideas. We'd love to hear from you—after all, we are publishing books for you!

Please stay in touch with us and follow us at:

Facebook: Mango Publishing
Twitter: @MangoPublishing
Instagram: @MangoPublishing
LinkedIn: Mango Publishing
Pinterest: Mango Publishing

Newsletter: mangopublishinggroup.com/newsletter

Join us on Mango's journey to reinvent publishing, one book at a time.